D1291331

English Costume
from the Early Middle Ages
through the Sixteenth Century

1250

English Costume
from the Early Middle Ages
through the Sixteenth Century

Iris Brooke

DOVER PUBLICATIONS, INC.
Mineola, New York

Bibliographical Note

This Dover edition, first published in 2000, is an unabridged republication of *English Costume of the Early Middle Ages: The Tenth to the Thirteenth Centuries,* originally published in 1936 by A. & C. Black, Ltd., London; and the following sections from *English Costume from the Fourteenth through the Nineteenth Century,* "English Costume of the Later Middle Ages: The Fourteenth and Fifteenth Centuries," and "English Costume in the Age of Elizabeth: The Sixteenth Century," originally published in 1937 by The Macmillan Company, New York. Aside from the new arrangement of material, the only other alteration consists in retaining the color plates in black and white in their original position in the books, as well as including them all in a separate full-color insert with page number references to the text they illustrate.

Library of Congress Cataloging-in-Publication Data

Brooke, Iris.
    [English costume of the early Middle Ages]
    English costume from the early Middle Ages through the sixteenth century / Iris Brooke.
       p. cm.
    Originally published: English costume of the early Middle Ages. London : A. & C. Black, 1936.
    Includes two sections from English costume from the fourteenth through the nineteenth century, originally published: New York : Macmillan Co., 1937.
    ISBN 0-486-41238-5 (pbk.)
    1. Costume—Great Britain—History. 2. Costume—History—Medieval, 500–1500. I. Brooke, Iris. English costume from the fourteenth through the nineteenth century. II. Title.

GT732 .B65 2000
391'.00942—dc21

00-031399

Manufactured in the United States of America
Dover Publications, Inc., 31 East 2nd Street, Mineola, N.Y. 11501

CONTENTS

FOREWORD

A S with the other books in this series, dealing with later costume, this must be taken only as a reasonably comprehensive guide to dress worn in this country from the 10th to the 13th century. Positive accuracy is clearly impossible in the reconstruction of clothes worn over one thousand years ago. It will be obvious that it is not practicable to arrange the groups of drawings in this book into short periods of years, as in the other books in this series; the drawings have therefore been arranged as accurately as possible in their probable sequence in four sections covering the four centuries with which the book is concerned.

Anglo-Saxon England was, it must be remembered, populated by a restless, warlike, and scattered people, perpetually harried by opposing forces, and clothes were little more than a necessary defence against the elements, the chief factor in dress being warmth and utility. It was not until well after the Conquest that costume became, in addition, a method of self-expression.

The Anglo-Saxon Chronicle and most of the later records of the period are concerned only with details of wars and battles, plagues and famines, harvests and even weather conditions, and, with almost the solitary exception of Matthew Paris, the chroniclers devote little or no space to clothes. The most useful source of information is to be found in the illuminated religious manuscripts in the British Museum and in numerous other libraries in this country and abroad; for the student with limited time at his disposal the British Museum has an excellent collection of originals and reproductions of practically all the most important contemporary works.

The 11th, 12th, and 13th centuries yield several contemporary ivories and chessmen, delicately carved and of exquisite workmanship, and these, together with the effigies and other relief carvings, are of far more technical value than any drawing, as they show in detail the line and flow of the draperies which played such an important part in the costume of that time. Indeed, during the 12th and 13th centuries the effigies had a naturalness that is not to be found in the more mannered sculptures of a later date.

The Bayeux Tapestry, of course, is also a useful source of pictorial information, but here again we must face the problem of lack of authentic dated records. In all probability this work was stretched over a great many years, and it is reasonable to surmise that it was not finished until at least a century after the Norman Conquest.

Alfred the Great, Canute, William the Conqueror, and Richard Cœur de Lion appear in these pages, and their costumes, simple in cut and design, are at once dignified and graceful, and form a striking contrast to the elaborate and fantastic costume of the later Middle Ages.

I. B.

PART I

English Costume
of the
Early Middle Ages
The Tenth to the Thirteenth Centuries

900—1000

ALTHOUGH the period with which this book is concerned begins with the tenth century, there were so few changes of costume during the Anglo-Saxon period that the first pages of drawings might equally apply to the two previous centuries.

From the scanty references to costume in the Anglo-Saxon Chronicle and other contemporary sources, it is evident that interest in costume was confined to its suitability as a covering and protection for the body. The only direction in which development was made was in the materials used, and great strides were made in weaving flax, wool, and even a little silk into fine materials. At this time all classes wore garments of practically the same type, and distinctions of rank were indicated by the richness of the material and the costliness of the personal decoration rather than by the form of the garments.

Ladies of high position spent much time in carding wool, spinning, and working with the needle. Embroidery was carried out in gold, silver, and coloured threads of silk and wool, and sometimes set with jewels. Many of the embroideries were of Byzantine design, an influence partly due to the introduction of a number of Greek weavers into the country.

9 0 0—1 0 0 0 (*continued*)

Women's garments at this time consisted of a loose outer gown or super tunic, cut fairly full and with wide sleeves reaching just below the elbow, but sometimes longer and turned back. Worn without a girdle, the gown was usually ankle-length but hitched up at the sides or front to about knee-length. Under this outer gown was worn another gown, long and full with sleeves tight at the wrist. Beneath this was worn another garment of the same shape, and the Anglo-Saxon name for this undermost garment was "smock." The cloaks worn by women were semicircular in shape and arranged so that the back portion was considerably longer than the front.

For the most part the colours of both men's and women's garments were the natural colours of the homespun materials, subdued colours such as greys and browns and bright blues, greens, and reds.

Ecclesiastical costume is not dealt with in this book, but as examples of embroidered garments are so few the designs on the priest's garments on the page facing are particularly interesting.

900—1000 *(continued)*

The usual foundation garment for men was cut on lines similar to modern pyjama trousers, and was known by the Anglo-Saxons as " bracco," and the Normans as " braies." Over the braies were worn cross-garterings, or the legs were bound from knee to ankle with leather thongs. These leg-bindings were very convenient for outdoor workers, and in a somewhat modified form have persisted through the centuries and are still worn by farm workers in some parts of the country to-day. Many of the people went barefoot with only their ankles bound.

During the tenth century few varieties of head-dress were worn by men except the helmet-shaped hat with a point at the top called a " Phrygian cap," the close-fitting cap and the plain gold coronet worn by people of rank. These three types of head-dress are illustrated on the opposite page.

Women's heads were always covered except in the cases of very young girls and slaves. Throughout this early period women's head-dresses were very simple and little variety can be found in the arrangement of the head-veil, the French name for which was " couvrechef" and the Anglo-Saxon " heafods-rægel " or head-rail. The first of the three examples illustrated is an arrangement for a very light fabric, as the weight of a heavy material would pull the loosely arranged folds off the head. The second head-dress shows a couvrechef of a smaller piece of material, with one end brought round and flung over the opposite shoulder. The last example was the most general manner of head-covering. Clasped beneath the chin with a brooch, it often hung in folds almost to the length of the gown itself, serving the double purpose of head-dress and cloak. This idea was often adopted by the men in colder weather, and their cloaks which were usually fastened at the shoulder were swung round so that the fastening was in front, and the cloak could then be easily drawn up over the head.

900—1000 (*continued*)

In addition to the foundation garment, the costume of an ordinary man consisted of a shirt, tunic, and cloak. The tunic was knee-length and belted or fastened tight at the waist. It was drawn on over the head and the neck opening was often fastened with a brooch. The tunics varied little except in the sleeves, which were sometimes close-fitting, cut several inches longer than the arm and pushed up over the wrist so that a corrugated effect was formed below the elbow. In other cases the sleeves were quite loose and reached only half-way down the forearm, disclosing the tightly-fitting shirt beneath. The upper classes wore bands of embroidery at the wrist or hem.

Cloaks were worn by all classes, and in shape were square, oblong, or semicircular, and similar to those worn by the women.

9 0 0—1 0 0 0 (*continued*)

The whole of the Anglo-Saxon period is one of struggle and unrest, and their preoccupation with war and conquest and the primitive state of their civilization explain the reasons for the slow development of costume. The tribes of Angles, Saxons, and Jutes in various parts of the country fought continually amongst themselves for supremacy. Eventually seven separate kingdoms emerged, but the struggle continued and out of these seven, three gained supremacy—Northumbria, Mercia, and Wessex, and in turn they exercised supremacy over each other. Under the pressure of the invasion from the North, Wessex gained a lasting dominion over the country, but although strong enough to check the invaders, the Danes were too strong to be expelled. At first the object of the Danes was plunder, but towards the middle of the ninth century their aim became settlement. Under Alfred a compromise was reached and the Danes agreed to remain within a specified part of the country known as the Danelaw. It was recaptured by Alfred's descendants, and England became a more united country.

Towards the end of the tenth century, however, Danish attacks recommenced, and after a period of misery and desolation under Ethelred the Unready, early in the eleventh century the country was finally captured by Canute, who was also king of Denmark and later of Norway, too. Under Canute's rule peace came to the country. Trade and commerce flourished not only between England and the king's Scandinavian dominions, but with the Mediterranean lands where the Danes and Norwegians had already penetrated.

Traders returned with the products of a more advanced civilization, silks and finely woven cloth, gems and costly metals and elaborate leather work, and from this time begins the slow but gradual development of costume into the fantastic raiment of the later Middle Ages.

1000—1100

THE figures on the page facing are taken from a drawing representing King Canute and his Queen, reputed to have been executed sometime between 1016 and 1020. There are one or two interesting innovations to note. The sleeves of the Queen's gown do not hang loose at the wrist, but are gathered in by a tight band, and the couvrechef is worn over a coronet. This custom seems to be confined to the early part of the eleventh century, although a later example may be seen in the figure on page 27, the date of which is approximately 1070.

The comparatively neat cut of the king's hair and beard shows a distinct advance on examples in earlier drawings. The beard and moustache are both well-trimmed and shaped, and the hair is cut short on the forehead and is allowed to curl slightly at the back. The hose are gartered at the top with a band of embroidery and cross-garterings are dispensed with. Another innovation is the ring on the cloak ; although not in use it seems quite clear that the two ends of the cloak were drawn through it, fastening the cloak at any desired height. Throughout this period swords were only worn on formal occasions and in times of war, and not as at a later date as an ornament.

I O O O—I I O O (*continued*)

The first figure on the opposite page shows the hose drawn up to the knee with a garter or band of embroidery at the top. The hose were of a loosely woven material and were pulled over the braies, which were made of white or coloured linen and reached the ankle. Cross-garterings and the puttee-like bindings were still worn during the first half of the century, but were not seen so much at the Conquest.

Shoes were a little more ornamental than previously, and as time went on were cut higher at the ankle until towards the end of the century they were more like a boot with a turned-down top. They were usually slit down the side or front and tied at the top or fastened with a buckle or brooch. The Anglo-Saxons had long understood the tanner's art, and a variety of leather was available for shoes. Undressed leather was used for rougher shoes, and dressed leather, often coloured and gilded, for the shoes of the wealthy. Cloth and felt were also used for shoes, and often embroidered and ornamented.

It will be seen that leg-wear consisted of three distinct items—the braies, the hose, and the shoes or boots. Short hose, made of leather or other material, were often worn over the hose, sometimes with and sometimes without shoes.

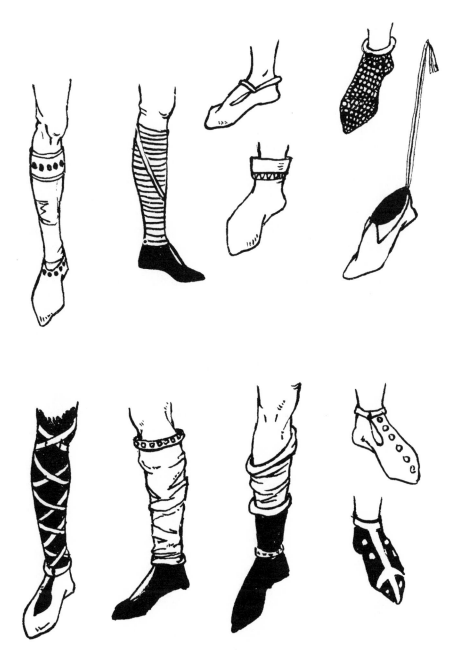

I O O O—I I O O (*continued*)

As garments at this time had no pockets, personal possessions such as keys, purses, and knives and daggers were suspended from the belt or girdle. Belts were sometimes worn under the tunic, and in the tight-fitting tunic at the bottom of the opposite page the sides have been slit to allow easy access, although as often the skirts of the tunic were cut full this was not necessary. If the belt was worn outside, the tunic was drawn up and allowed to flop over, thus hiding the belt itself.

In some tunics of this time, as on page 31, there is a band of embroidery at the waist or above it. This is part of the ornamentation of the gown similar to the bands of embroidery at the neck and elbow and should not be confused with the belt. In this example the belt was worn under the tunic. The garments worn by both men and women at this time were extremely simple in cut and design. The lower half of the man's garment was practically a half-circle, so that the skirt of the tunic was very full, and if the tunic was long it was almost pleated in its fullness. The women's tunics were not cut on such a generous scale, but their fullness gave little scope for displaying the figure. It was not until the twelfth century that women's garments began to develop into the revealing garments of later periods.

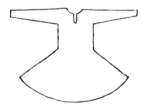

I O O O—I I O O (*continued*)

It was during the second half of the eleventh century that linings to gowns and cloaks were first used to any extent. The linings were usually of a contrasting colour, although the wealthy occasionally used fur. Borders of embroidery or appliqued designs were more popular than earlier in the century and for the most part followed simple geometrical designs.

Cloaks were worn in a variety of ways, and sometimes, as on the page facing, after the Roman manner. These cloaks were cut in a circular pattern; some were simply a half-circle of material with a large ring sewn at one side of the neck through which the other side of the cloak was pulled, as in the first drawing on page 29. They were cut in a variety of lengths varying from knee to ankle, and were sometimes worn with a metal or stiffly ornamented collar.

It is often impossible to find out how garments at this early age were made. Contemporary chroniclers found no space to describe the costumes of the age, and the crudeness of the drawings available and the carelessness of the copyists make many of them of little value.

I O O O—I I O O (*continued*)

This set of drawings shows the fusion of the costume of the tenth and eleventh centuries. The first figure wears his braies tight-fitting almost like hose and unbound, with his buskins, the gauntlet-topped boots covering the ankle. This fashion is only found between the middle of the eleventh century and the end of the twelfth. At the bottom of the page is an example of cross-gartering which was still to be seen. The motif design on the skirts of this man's tunic is often seen in contemporary drawings. Any part of the garment might be embroidered and it was not considered necessary to maintain the same decorative scheme throughout. Often the bands of embroidery at the neck, arms, and border of a tunic are of different designs, and in the tunic illustrated three distinct designs are used. It is interesting to note, however, in the illustrations of the time, that the same designs constantly appear. The embroiderers' lack of originality and initiative was perhaps compensated by the delicacy and finish of their work, for which they were renowned on the Continent.

It is probable that the bands of embroidery lasted many years and were transferred from one garment to another. The tasselled tie at the throat of the tunic is an interesting variation from the usual brooch. The square neck-line gradually became as popular as the older round style.

I O O O—I I O O (*continued*)

The Danish supremacy had very little immediate effect on costume in England, and to an extent Canute's followers adopted the customs and dress of the English. It is interesting to find, however, that their ideas of cleanliness were in advance of the English. They paid more attention to personal appearance, and they combed their hair at least once a day, bathed once a week and often changed their attire. Although the English looked on these habits as effeminate, their wives and daughters were not slow to approve, and the Danes were popular with the fairer sex.

During the short interval between the Danish and Norman conquests, when the English throne reverted to the Saxon line, there is little to record except the complaint of William of Malmesbury that in the time of Edward the Confessor the English had transformed themselves into Frenchmen and Normans. Edward had spent his life in exile at the Court of Normandy, and it was natural that his sympathies should have been with their manners and customs. William complained that the English not only adopted the Norman strange way of speaking and behaviour, but also their absurdly short tunics, their clipped hair and their mode of hairdressing.

The diagram below indicates how the man's tunic is cut. It will be seen that the top part of the tunic is triangular, with a hole cut out for the head. At a later date the sleeves were even fuller at the base and carried on from the waist itself.

I O O O—I I O O (*continued*)

For the most part men wore their hair to the tips of the
ears with a fringe in front, and although at the Conquest
the Normans were closely-cropped and shaved their heads,
they soon adopted the English fashion.

Three forms of the Phrygian cap are illustrated on the
page facing. With few exceptions this was almost the only
type of head-dress worn by men during the eleventh century.
Several examples of the simple conical hat illustrated on the
opposite page may be found in the Cotton MS. Claudius B IV.
This manuscript, which may be seen in the British Museum,
well repays study. The colours are brilliant and beautiful
and the patterns more varied than in any one manuscript of
the period. The drawings themselves, and especially the
unfinished ones, have a spontaneity not often found at this
early date. Other useful manuscripts in the Cotton collection
include the MSS. Tiberius, Caligula, and Cleopatra. The
last contains many costumes that are not really of this period,
although Cleopatra appears swathed from head to toe in
voluminous garments of the eleventh century.

It will be seen that women's heads were still covered and
their head-dresses differed hardly at all from those worn
several centuries earlier. The last figure has her couvrechef
cut with a semicircular front which gives a goffered effect ;
another example of this is given on page 41.

1 0 0 0—1 1 0 0 *(continued)*

The Norman Conquest had little immediate effect on costume. William of Malmesbury says that the Normans were splendidly dressed, but this refers more to the materials than to the design of their costumes.

When times of peace came hundreds of French craftsmen and domestics came over and settled round the new castles built by the Norman nobles on the land presented to them by the King and round the new churches built by the ecclesiastics from the Continent. Around the Abbey of Battle, for instance, there were Gilbert the Foreigner, Gilbert the Weaver, Benet the Steward, Hugh the Secretary, and Baldwin the Tailor. In the large towns there was a steady influx of traders from France, and all the fineries of the Continent and East, the silks and finely woven materials and personal luxuries, such as gloves and shoes, became available to those who could afford them. Many of these traders had already established business connections with the English in the time of Edward the Confessor, but now they came to settle in earnest, and thus began the slow blending of the conquerors and conquered into one people.

Towards the end of the century, in the reign of William Rufus, the nobles had become wealthy at the expense of the English, and the whole period, not only as regards costume, is one of extravagance. Fashions for the most part remained unaltered, but the materials were costly and decorated to an absurd degree. William of Malmesbury is moved to write " then was the time of flowing locks and extravagant dress, then came in the fashion of shoes with curved points ; then it was the correct thing for young men to outdo women in effeminacy."

The Bayeux Tapestry, believed to have been made at the request of Bishop Odo, half-brother of William I, is an interesting source of information for details of the period, although the exact date of its execution is uncertain. Embroidered in coloured wools on a background of coarse linen, it sets forth in great detail the history of the Conquest. Most of the costumes are naturally military in character, and the English soldiers are shown wearing Norman equipment.

I O O O—I I O O (*continued*)

Men's leg-wear changed considerably during the twelfth century. Loose braies gradually went out of fashion and braies fitting close to the leg were adopted. For centuries the hose had barely reached the knee, but during the first quarter of the century they became longer and often the braies were cut shorter and tucked into the top of the hose. A garment similar to modern shorts was popular in this century. They varied in length, some being like running shorts, with the tunic or shirt tucked into the top, and others much longer and more like the Norfolk breeches worn in the early years of the twentieth century. In all cases the legs were covered, either with the long hose or the tight-fitting braies.

The skirts of the tunic were tucked up in a variety of ways, as illustrated in several of the drawings devoted to this century. Sometimes the hose were rolled down to just above the knee, and it is probable that the band of embroidery at the top of the hose was used as a kind of garter and not merely as an ornament. Men's tunics were worn long and heavily ornamented at this time. The hair and beard were worn long and were carefully combed.

I I O O—I 2 O O

THE first three figures on the page facing are typical costumes of the beginning of the twelfth century. The three at the bottom of the page are all of the eleventh century.

Here may be seen the first example of a woman of high station wearing a train to her gown, the sleeves of which are cut very wide and short and lined with a contrasting colour.

A great change in the appearance of women in this century was in the arrangement of the hair, which is said to be due to Matilda, wife of Henry I. The Queen was an Anglo-Saxon princess, and incidentally it is through her that the present royal family of England is directly descended from Alfred the Great. For over a century women's hair had been concealed beneath head-cloths, and it must have been a welcome relief when the new fashion of displaying the hair was introduced. The hair had previously been plaited in two plaits wound round the head and completely covered by the head-dress. With the appearance of the hair feminine competition begins in earnest, and women outdid each other in the length and thickness of the plaits which now hung down their backs. Artificial hair was introduced, and later the fashion was carried to extremes and the plaits encased in silken cases reached the ground.

Matilda fostered many of the old Anglo-Saxon accomplishments with which ladies of high station had formerly employed themselves, and Norman ladies at the Court followed the Queen's example in spinning, weaving, and embroidery. Some of the ladies worked in their dairies, milking and churning, and the Countess of Chester was famous for her cheese-making.

1 1 0 0—1 2 0 0 (*continued*)

The figures on the opposite page are taken from a contemporary carving on ivory, and the costumes show the changes that took place in the early years of the twelfth century. The woman wears her loose-sleeved gown over the more tightly fitting under-tunic, the skirt of which is cut circular so that it falls in a profusion of folds at the bottom. Bands of embroidery are worn at the waist, the wrists, and the hem of the outer garment. Women's cloaks are not often seen fastened together in front at this date, and the method illustrated in the drawing of fastening the cloak with cords and tassels became very popular, revealing as it does the more interesting neck-line of the gown. The veil is semicircular in cut with the straight edge worn at the back and the curved edge forming a frill on the brow.

The man's costume shows a most interesting innovation in male attire. The outer or super tunic is the usual Norman tunic but it is now worn over a full undertunic which reaches the ground. The wide bands of embroidery on the supertunic are typical of the time. Sometimes they are worked straight, or, as in this case, diagonally; the single band was more often seen than a repeating design.

The manner of cutting on the circle forms the basis of all the fullness of garments at this time. It will be noticed that the man's cloak appears fuller at the front point, and it is likely that this additional fullness was obtained by cutting the cloak as illustrated in the sketch below. The two V-shaped additions to the semicircle give an added grace to the fullness.

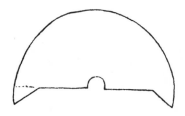

I I O O—I 2 O O (*continued*)

There was a tendency towards individuality in clothes during this century. The long-established forms of arrangement, cut, and shape were no longer strictly adhered to, and the clothes of both men and women began to show signs of personal taste and preference. More originality was displayed in the design of patterns, and sleeves were more varied. The length of the sleeves on the supertunic might be merely a few inches in length and finished with a broad band of embroidery, with the contrasting and tightly-fitting sleeve of the tunic beneath reaching to the wrist, or they might be quite full but fitting to the wrist with a cuff of some contrasting material or embroidery.

From about 1120 women discarded the heavily draped head-veil and a lighter and altogether smaller one took its place. In the case of a lady of quality a coronet was worn over the head-dress.

The mode for longer hair was adopted by the men and carefully combed locks and beards took the place of the short or ear-length cut of the early years of the century. The beards appear to have been dressed with wax of some sort. They were neatly parted and curled in a symmetrical pattern, not unlike the beard-dressing of the Assyrians centuries earlier. The hair was usually cut with a long curled fringe which was plastered down on the forehead in an arrangement of curls, curling outward from the centre. It was worn in ringlets reaching to just below the shoulders, and sometimes it was longer with the ends forming a loose loop of curl. These extremes of fashion and others equally absurd may be seen in contemporary drawings of royal functions and were of course only adopted by the Court. The ordinary man continued to wear his hair cut fairly short all round.

I I O O—I 2 O O (*continued*)

One important change in the appearance of women has already been noted ; another even more important change was the adoption of a close-fitting gown, cut to fit the body tightly down to the hips. Many of these gowns can be seen in the effigies of the period, and they appear to have been worn over a corset of some sort. Few details are available of the exact form this undergarment took, and it is possible that the desired effect of reducing the size of the waist was achieved by a wide band of material or leather sewn tightly round the body. The earliest example in this country of a corset with lacings may be found in an illuminated manuscript of the British Museum, Nero, C.iv, which was completed about 1265. The drawing shows a devil wearing tight-laced corsets, knotted skirts and sleeves and other absurdities of the times.

Yet another change in women's fashions was the new sleeve. Many of these were cut in a bell shape, and others were fairly tight-fitting to the wrist, where a deep band of embroidery formed a gigantic hanging cuff. Towards the end of the century they became so large that they were knotted to save them dragging along the ground. An example of this may be seen on page 57.

The embroidered or otherwise ornamented neckline and the girdle are two other fashions popular at the beginning of the century. Early examples of the girdle were composed of silk and silver and gold threads ornamented with beads. The girdle was worn round the waist, crossed at the back and tied loosely in front below the hips, the tasselled and jewelled ends hanging almost to the hem of the gown.

I I O O—I 2 O O (*continued*)

Men's belts or girdles assumed a new importance, and many examples show a marked sense of individuality. Previously, belts had served the useful purpose of holding in a loose gown, or carrying the purse, but now they became an object of ornamentation to the super-tunic. They were usually four or five feet in length and made of leather or precious metals. One end was finished with a buckle or a large metal ring and the other tapered and hung down in front of the tunic. The belts worn by the wealthy were costly ; sometimes the whole belt was embroidered or studded with stones and in some examples the ornamentation is confined to the portion near the buckle.

The simple spot patterns of earlier times became less popular as the century advanced. The diaper patterns, those founded on a large chequered ground with a geometrical design within each square, were used extensively throughout the century. Another type of design favoured by the nobility was the large repeating motif between lines or bands of embroidery, examples of which may be found throughout the twelfth and thirteenth centuries. In many contemporary drawings a single motif may be seen embroidered on the garment. It is possible that this was representative of an all-over pattern, as the drawings at this period were so mannered that even furs were represented in heraldic style and everything was simplified in its pictorial representation. The bands of embroidery worn on the garments at this time are represented so stiffly that it is probable that they were set with jewels on a groundwork of fine metal mesh. Even the lighter bands of embroidery have the appearance of stiff tapestry and all of them are enriched with beads or precious stones.

I I O O—I 2 O O (*continued*)

The drawing from which the illustration on the page facing is taken may be found in the John the Baptist Roll. The colours in this Roll are clear and are beautifully preserved and, what is rare at this time, there is a variety in the clothes depicted. It is interesting to note in most cases the artist seems to have used one model for all the figures depicted.

The parti-coloured super-tunic is one of the earliest examples in existence. The fashion for parti-coloured clothing lasted in varying degrees of popularity from about 1150 until well into the sixteenth century. Sometimes the hose were of the same colour, but more often they were of contrasting colours as illustrated here. It is worthy of note that this is one of the few fashions confined to men, as there are no instances where a woman is seen wearing a parti-coloured gown.

At this time women wore their hair in a variety of ways. Plaits were most popular ; several examples of four plaits may be seen, two worn at the back and two over the shoulders. Sometimes these were bound with silk and not plaited but held together by a complicated method of twisting silken ribands around the tresses.

In the last years of the century the crespine was introduced. This was a net, often of gold mesh, which enclosed the hair. Another new head-dress was the barbette, or band worn under the chin and joined on the top of the head. Introduced by Eleanor, wife of Henry II, it was worn until well into the fourteenth century.

An example of the barbette will be seen at the bottom of page 55, and it is worn with a circular veil over the head and a crown. It will be noticed that there are a great many representations of crowns and coronets in these pages, and it should be remembered that they were worn, as they are still worn on state occasions to-day, by bearers of rank.

I I O O—I 2 O O (*continued*)

Two examples of the girdle or belt are given at the bottom of the page. The first is an interesting arrangement of the knotted girdle worn by a woman. The silken cords are brought through the square buckle and tied in a large knot, and the cord hanging in front is ornamented at intervals with large beads or gems. The second is an example of a man's belt, also with a square buckle. Most belts at this time, however, have circular buckles.

The extensive use of rings as a means of fastening garments at this time even extended to the footwear. On the leg with the dark hose will be seen a boot, with the very full gauntlet top drawn tightly through a ring above the ankle. Boots were far more popular during this century than before and shoes were cut in far greater variety. Long-toed, short-toed, embossed and embroidered, they were sometimes open at the instep but more often closed and reaching well over the ankle. The shoe itself was not often embroidered and separate bands of embroidery were sewn on. Another means of ornamentation was to sew small rings of gold and silver, sometimes even on to the toe and heel of the shoe, and some shoes were covered with fine gold mesh. In some instances gems or beads are sewn on to the gold mesh.

At the top of the page facing is an example of a boot split up the side and laced tightly to fit the leg. Lacing was probably also used for the shorter boot when it was tight-fitting, although few drawings show the details of the fastening.

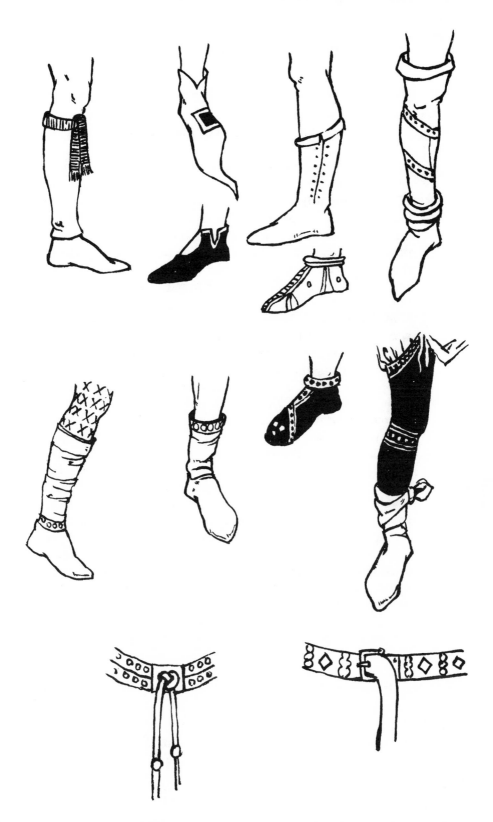

I I O O—I 2 O O (*continued*)

During the last twenty years of the twelfth century it appears from contemporary works, an exceptional number of which are still in existence, that on the whole costume was still fairly simple in design although rich in stuffs and ornamentation. The collars worn on the tunic or super-tunic were more intricate in design, and in some instances they are more like small shoulder capes and not attached to the tunic. The cloak was still semicircular in cut and frequently lined with fur.

Men's hats of this period are particularly interesting. They were ornamented in a variety of ways and often with jewels. It will be noticed that they nearly all finish with a point or tuft at the top, and on those made of soft woollen materials the tuft resembles that on a modern beret. Some of the hats had spikes on top, which may have been useful in removing the hat as the brim was negligible. A wider brimmed hat was worn by the peasantry to protect them from the heat of the sun as they worked in the fields, but otherwise the hats were all small with a mere roll as a brim. Hoods were still worn a great deal ; in some cases they were attached to the cloak but often were a quite separate head covering. Shepherds' cloaks always included a hood.

The woman's gown at the bottom of the page shows the extreme shaping typical of this period. The long sleeves must have swept the ground unless the wearer's arms were raised. A simple contrasting border of material is the only ornament besides the girdle, which is of the plainest design. It is interesting to note that these extremely voluminous sleeves were not adopted by men until a couple of centuries later, and in this case at anyrate the old adage of man aping woman is reversed.

I I O O—I 2 O O (*continued*)

During the twelfth century the Phrygian cap dwindled and degenerated into a caricature of its original form. It is even possible that the curious little cap resembling the cap of an acorn, including its stalk, was a parody of the Phrygian cap. Men's head-dresses can be divided into three groups: the caps already mentioned, the wide-brimmed straw hat of the peasant, and the hood. The brimmed hats were usually conical in shape, and it will be seen from the first head in the second row of drawings that hardly any line occurred where the brim left off and the crown began. A hat consisting of a crown and a brim was not introduced until the following century, and the hat which appears to have a brim at this time was really a hat with the crown elongated so that it gave protection to the eyes and neck.

The hood was worn by all classes, either as a separate item or attached to the tunic, super-tunic, or gown. Following the tendencies of the time, the hoods were usually cut with a slight point at the top.

The three methods of women's hair-dressing illustrated here have all been dealt with. The last is interesting as the earliest example of the crespine or hair-net, and is taken from a panel carved during the last five years of the century. It shows that the hair was worn in " shells " over the ears and not worn in a bun at the back as it was in the following century.

I I O O—I 2 O O (*continued*)

During the reign of Stephen from 1135 to 1154 the country was too disturbed by wars and battles for much development in costume, and in the reign of his successor, Henry II, costumes were still plain in design but richer in materials.

Remembering the enmity between the King and Thomas à Becket, it is interesting to find that early in the reign William Fitzstephen says that " never were any two men more absolute friends in Christian times." The King and the Chancellor, as Becket then was, were out riding one day, and seeing a poor man approaching them the King asks if it would not be a real charity to give him a thick warm cloak. Becket replies that it would, and the King should do it. The King jokingly replies that Becket should do so and in friendly jest attempts to pull off the Chancellor's fine new scarlet cloak. Becket resists the attempt, but finally gives way and the poor man receives the cloak.

The popularity of the tight-fitting garments, almost jersey-like in their clinging lines, did not last throughout the century, and they were superseded by more loosely-fitting garments, belted at the waist and often so generously cut that the folds hung over the belt or girdle. This fashion remained in general use until the tight-fitting cotehardie was introduced in the fourteenth century.

The woman's dress illustrated on the opposite page shows traces of both fashions—it is looser but it still retains the clinging lines of earlier years.

I I O O—I 2 O O (*continued*)

Richard I, who came to the throne in 1189, had little influence on costume. Most of his short reign of ten years was occupied with the Crusades, and of this time he spent only eight months in England and his wife Berengaria never visited the country at all. The King was not slow to take advantage of his position in raising money for his expeditions. Everything was put up for sale—offices, lordships, earldoms, shrievalties, castles, towns and estates, and it is recorded that Bishop Hugh of Durham gave the King a thousand silver marks to be Justiciar of England and be excused from the Crusade.

"Let no love of earthly possessions detain you," said Pope Urban II, exhorting the faithful to free Jerusalem from the Turks, and although religious fervour undoubtedly inspired many of the followers of Peter the Hermit in the first Crusade at the end of the eleventh century and the Crusaders of the twelfth century, they were a very mixed crowd, and many of them were out for plunder. The Crusaders who returned home brought with them the spoils and profits of battle, including dresses and tunics of brilliant colouring and Eastern design, and it is interesting to find that the garments of both men and women at this time show traces of Oriental influence. Garments were looser and fuller, sleeves wider, and embroidery more elaborate. In the following century the influence increased rather than diminished as the century proceeded.

1200—1300

THERE were no remarkable changes in men's costume in the thirteenth century. A large cloak or mantle with ample sleeves and a variety of caps and hats, often of fantastic shapes, were worn, and are illustrated in the succeeding pages. Women's costume appears to have altered very little during the first part of the century. The long and inconvenient sleeves of the reigns of Henry I and Stephen had gone out of fashion before the accession of John in 1199, and the only addition to feminine apparel appears to have been a garment called a " Pelisson " or pelice, and a chin or neck-cloth called a wimple. King John ordered a grey pelisson with nine bars of fur to be made for the Queen, but apart from the fact that it was a winter garment there are no identifiable examples.

A word may be said here concerning cloaks. The cloaks or mantles worn by the Danes and the Normans in the eleventh century were almost identical, and from contemporary illustrations it is seen that the cloaks of Canute and his wife and William the Conqueror are fastened in a similar manner by cords or laces with tassels. Henry II is said to have introduced a shorter cloak than those previously worn, several examples of which may be seen in the preceding pages. From the latter half of the twelfth century and onwards there is a great variety of cloaks and mantles, and the writers of the times describe them by many different names—the capa, the caputium, the rheno, the super-totus, the balandrana, to mention only a few. It is not possible to trace the distinction between them, and we only know that they were cloaks worn during this period. Many of them were lined with silk or lighter materials for summer wear, and with fur for winter wear, as in the drawing on the opposite page. Those of the wealthy were embroidered and ornamented lavishly.

I 2 0 0—I 3 0 0 (*continued*)

Striped and patterned materials became more popular as the century advanced, and in the drawing of the common soldier at the top of the page facing, not only is his super-tunic striped, but his hose also are ornamented with bands and spots. The sleeves of his garment show the added fullness at the base which often stretched from the waist of the garment to the shoulder. The skirt is split at the front, although in many cases they were split at the sides. Some-times the garments were " dagged," as in the figure at the bottom of the page. One noticeable and lasting effect of the Crusades on fashion was that of shorter cut hair. Long and elaborately curled hair was found to be unsuitable by the Crusaders for their journeys in warmer lands, and thus the shorter mode was introduced and remained the most popular style during the thirteenth century.

Quite early in the century the coif, a close-fitting hat for the head, became popular, and it is possible that this also was introduced by the Crusaders. It was often worn under the head-covering of mail, to protect the head perhaps from the reflected heat of the sun on the mail. In illustrations of the reign of Henry III it is represented white, apparently of linen, and tied under the chin like a child's nightcap. It was worn by all classes, and on the heads of huntsmen, knights in armour, and men in action it has a ludicrous appearance. Most of the costumes on the opposite page are of the middle years of the reign of Henry III.

The shaped but sleeveless gown of the woman on the opposite page is an early example of a fashion which reached the height of its popularity in the following century, and is the forerunner of the cotehardie of the fourteenth and fifteenth centuries.

I 2 0 0—I 3 0 0 (*continued*)

The garment worn by the man in the illustration on the opposite page is taken from an effigy of King John, and shows the Dalmatic, a loose-fitting garment with very wide sleeves, full skirts and belted at the waist. Primarily an ecclesiastical garment, its use was later conceded to emperors and kings at their coronation and when assisting at High Mass. In the account of John's coronation robes it is mentioned as being of a dark purple colour. The stiff gold collar is heavily ornamented with jewels of so large a size that one would doubt their reality if it were not for jewels of a similar nature still reposing in the treasuries of several cathedrals on the Continent and which at one time ornamented priestly vestments. The precious stones mostly used in this century include topazes of almost unbelievable size, emeralds, garnets, sapphires, rubies, diamonds, amethysts, amber, and rock crystal.

John was extravagant in dress but he introduced no new styles or fashions and was content to wear the designs of the previous century, but decorated in a costly or showy manner.

Gloves were an important part of a king's dress, and it will be noticed that in the illustration the back of the King's glove, which was probably made of kid or calfskin, is studded with a precious stone. Gloves do not appear to have been worn in England before the beginning of the eleventh century, and it is interesting to note that no gloves are visible in the Bayeux Tapestry, not even on the hands of Harold, who in one section is seen carrying a hawk. The early gloves were bag-shaped, and gloves with fingers were not introduced until the twelfth century. One of the earliest examples of this kind is seen on an effigy of Henry II.

I 2 O O — I 3 O O (*continued*)

Mention has not yet been made of a garment first introduced by the Crusaders in the twelfth century as a part of military attire, but which later achieved wider popularity and became a part of civil attire. This garment was the surcoat or surcote, and in many respects it resembled the super-tunic, and indeed is often referred to as such. Its main purpose was to protect the armour of the Crusaders from the weather, from the rain as one authority asserts, but more probably from the rays of the Syrian sun which heated it excessively. This surcoat descended in folds to the knee, was without sleeves and usually open at the front or sides. A soldier at the top of page 87 is wearing one of this type over his hauberk or coat of mail. The surcoats sometimes had the distinguishing red cross, but often the heraldic device of a noble. The surcoat is also the name given to a garment worn over the tight-fitting garment or cote worn by women which superseded the tunic during part of this century. The super-tunic was the garment worn by both sexes over another tunic, and is to be seen in great variety in this century. Sometimes they were knee-length, but often almost as long as the under-tunic; they were worn full and otherwise, with openings at the sides or front. The sleeves vary in length and design.

An interesting garment is illustrated at the bottom of the page facing. It was an outer garment, loosely fitting and unbelted, hanging from the shoulder to the calf or ankle and with very full sleeves. The sleeves were slit at the elbow so that the hand might come out, and sometimes this slit extended almost to the end of the sleeve. These garments were lined with a contrasting material and sometimes worn with a hood attached. Another example is illustrated on page 69, and in this case the garment has a large fur collar cut to fit tightly over the shoulder.

1 2 0 0—1 3 0 0 (*continued*)

The long reign of Henry III, from 1216 until 1272, is referred to by historians as a period of extravagance, but it will be seen from the preceding pages of drawings and in those which follow that as far as the form of costume is concerned it is not so, and extravagance is confined to the materials used and to ornamentation.

Many and rare costly materials were used at this time. Damask, a rich description of figured satin or linen, received its name from the city of Damascus where it was presumably first manufactured. In a romance of the period, *The Squire of Low Degree*, there is a reference to it :

> Damask white and azure blewe,
> Well diapered with lillies new.

Velvet, or vellet as it is sometimes referred to in the thirteenth century, was occasionally used for garments, including the mantles of the Knights Templars. Another material used was baldekin or baudekyn, a costly stuff of silk and gold, so called because it was originally manufactured at Baldech, one of the names of Babylon or Baghdad. It was used for robes of state, canopies and curtains, and Matthew Paris speaks of it in 1247 as forming part of the royal vestments of Henry III when he conferred the honour of knighthood on William de Valence.

Other materials used were samite, a stuff wholly of silk, but frequently interwoven with gold and silver and embroidered in a lavish manner ; cendal, a silken stuff used not only for garments but for flags, horse-trappings, and curtains. The celebrated banner of St. Denis is said to have been made of " cendal pur." Tissue and cloths of gold and silver were also much used, and silk had become quite common and was used extensively.

1 2 0 0—1 3 0 0 (*continued*)

The next page of drawings has been devoted to the costumes worn by the poorer classes in this century. The first figure is wearing a loose tunic over a shirt and what may be described as breeches or drawers. They were probably split at the sides as in the figure beneath, and for convenience the ends were knotted together. The third figure shows the tunic gathered up at the waist, and similar examples are to be found in the two previous centuries. It is not clear how this was done, unless the folds were tucked into the belt worn beneath.

The old man with the stick is wearing a hood with a loose cape. Countrywomen wore long loose gowns with or without a simple girdle. The villages were self-supporting and the peasants spun their own coarse cloth from wool and hemp. The natural wool-coloured garments were often dyed with natural dyes—bright blues, reds and greens.

Many of the peasants went barefoot when working in wet or marshy land, but at times wore shoes made of rough tanned leather or black cloth.

1 2 0 0—1 3 0 0 (*continued*)

The crespine, the net for confining the hair, has already been described, and several examples are given in the preceding pages. The barbette, to which reference has also been made, the crespine and the fillet were the three main factors in head-dresses. The fillet was the band worn round the head and was usually made of stiff linen varying in width from one and a half to three inches. It was always worn with either the crespine or barbette and more often both. Sometimes the upper edge was serrated, sometimes goffered or cut in points. It was not always composed of net, and sometimes a plain material was used to tuck away the hair. The hair was worn either plaited or loose or even tied into a large loose bun at the back.

A flat-topped bonnet something like a pill-box in shape was introduced soon after Henry III came to the throne. The illustrations on the page facing show the variety of ways in which these head-dresses were worn. On the third head, instead of the more usual fillet, the barbette is worn with a veil wound round the head. The head immediately beneath it shows a useful way of disposing of the veil when working. It is loosely wound round the head and tied in front, giving a turban-like effect.

I 2 O O—I 3 O O (*continued*)

The first figure on the page facing represents a common soldier of the time donning his coat of mail, and although armour is not included within the scope of this book, a few examples have been inserted to show how the coats of mail were connected with the other garments worn in the thirteenth century. In this case the tunic, tight-sleeved but full-skirted, is split at the front to give as much play and freedom as possible. Independent thigh coverings were worn over the hose and tied to the waist in the same manner as the hose. The coif is worn under the metal head-covering.

The next figure shows a countrywoman with her gown split at the sides like an apron and showing an undertunic beneath. By this time gloves were worn for rough work in the fields. The two women's gowns at the bottom of the page are earlier examples of the garment described on page 78 ; in both cases the sleeves are attached to the shoulder so that they may be worn in either of the ways depicted. The method of tying the sleeves in a knot behind was easier than rolling the sleeves back from the wrist, as in most cases the sleeves were tight-fitting. One of the women is wearing striped hose, a fashion only rarely adopted by women.

The pouch hanging from the waist of the other woman is interesting. It is closed at the top by means of two cords and is covered with a fine mesh work, the bottom being ornamented with beads. Another example will be found on page 65.

All the drawings on the opposite page are taken from the Bible Moralise, one of the most interesting and informative illuminated manuscripts of the thirteenth century. It is a particularly valuable record of costume of about 1260 or a little later, as it shows not only the clothes of royalty and the nobility, but of every class, including peasants and the common soldiers.

I 2 0 0—I 3 0 0 (*continued*)

The two costumes on the page facing show a milkmaid and shepherd of the middle of the thirteenth century. The milkmaid is far from being poorly clad ; her dress is simple though quite in accordance with the prevailing fashions, and her cloak is lined with a contrasting colour. Her head-dress is of the approved mode, but her hair is not confined in a crespine, being loosely knotted at the back. There is little difference between her attire and that of the ladies at the bottom of the following page of illustrations, and only the milk pail indicates her calling.

The dress of her companion, on the other hand, is nothing like the garments worn by his master. The short but full tunic is well adapted to his work, and his hood with the sheepskin cape attached, although picturesque is strictly utilitarian. The highcut shoes and the leg-bindings hardly differ from those worn centuries earlier. The working man of the thirteenth century is not often seen wearing hose, either his legs are covered with braies or short hose or bound with leather, and usually he went barefoot.

I 2 O O—I 3 O O (*continued*)

The second figure illustrated on the opposite page is wearing a garment similar to those worn by the women at the bottom of page 75. It was worn fairly short, and in this instance is split at the front and has no belt or girdle. Pelice is the Norman-French word for fur, and fur-lined gowns of many varieties are referred to as pelissons. Fur was used a great deal at this time both for lining and trimming. Among the furs used were ermine, sable, squirrel, marten, minevair, which was probably pure white ermine without tails or spots and very costly, and vair, which seems to have been a composite fur available in several forms. The fur of a species of squirrel or weasel, which was grey on the back and white on the throat and belly, was also called vair.

Although the tunic of the last figure on the page is simple and of the usual cut, the collar and cuff strike a new note in decoration. In the manuscript from which it is taken they are both represented in gold. It is possible that they were made of leather painted gold, or even cloth of gold, although its use was usually confined to dresses for state and ceremonial occasions. The use of gold leaf is so lavish in manuscripts at this time that the artist may have erred on the side of accuracy in the interests of pictorial decoration.

I 2 O O—I 3 O O (*continued*)

The grotesque exaggeration of the barbette and fillet at the bottom of the page is taken from an illustration which represents the hair encased in a sort of green bag. The fillet is a gem-studded coronet. This lady's cloak is fastened in an interesting manner, as the cord which holds the two sides together has ornamented buckles, one of which is adjustable, and thus permitting the cloak to be worn in a variety of ways. The next figure shows the plaits encased in long silken tubes bound or ornamented with gold or silver cord. The three little beaded tassels at the ends of the tubes are often seen in examples of this fashion. After about the middle of the century the fashion for plaits was largely superseded by the fillet and crespine. The crespine was worn in a variety of ways and made of many different materials, from those made of gold or silver net and studded with jewels worn by the wealthy and descending in splendour to the plain linen or net covering worn by countrywomen. In some cases the hair within was worn at the sides, but often it was worn at the back.

I 2 O O—I 3 O O (*continued*)

When Edward I came to the throne in 1272, the fashions of Henry III's reign remained unaltered, except that garments became even simpler. Queen Eleanor followed her husband's example, and the costumes of this reign are the simplest in the history of this country. But although the clothes were so simple they were dignified and graceful, especially cloaks, which were worn in a variety of ways. Unnecessary trimmings and ornaments were abandoned, but costly materials were still used, and it is recorded that a hundred lords and ladies " clad all in silk " sat at the Round Table at Kenilworth. It was the King's aim to be the model of the fashionable French notions of chivalry of the time, and one of his attempts was to renew the faded glories of the Court of King Arthur.

Gowns were cut full and long and hung in folds at the feet, and, as will be noticed in the woman's gown at the bottom of the opposite page, girdles were not worn. Towards the end of the century the skirt of the outer gown is so ample as to form a train, and it is interesting to read that this fashion was condemned by the moralists of the time. Robert de Brunne in his *Handlyng Sinne* writes of the wickedness of wearing trains, and tells at length the story of how two monks saw a woman with a devil sitting on the end of her train.

1 2 0 0—1 3 0 0 (*continued*)

Men's head-dresses continue in great variety, and it will be seen in the drawings on the opposite page that several of them show the influence of the East. The hats with the turned-up brims appear fairly frequently in the second half of the century and were made of felt or cloth.

During the reign of Edward I the hood began to develop in a curious fashion. The peak of the hood grew longer, and by the end of the reign it was often three feet in length. Its subsequent development is described and illustrated in a companion book to the present volume which deals with the costume of the Later Middle Ages.

The popularity of the coif, the tight-fitting bonnet illustrated in the last drawing, remained undiminished. It is interesting to find that in the reign of Henry III priests were forbidden to wear the coif except when travelling, as it was alleged that the disguise it afforded often resulted in priests forgetting their priestly functions.

Many men at this time followed the French fashion of being clean-shaven. Beards and moustaches were still worn, however, and received careful attention.

I 2 0 0—I 3 0 0 (*continued*)

It will be seen from the drawings on the page facing that often the whole body, from head to foot and the tips of the fingers, was encased in armour of some form or other. Over the hauberk, or coat of mail, was worn a surcoat, which in the twelfth century was quite plain or embroidered with gold or silver, but in the thirteenth century became more elaborate and ornamented with heraldic devices. A belt, often richly ornamented, was worn round the waist and from it hung the sword. The sleeves of the hauberk usually extended beyond the wrist and covered the hands, which could be slipped out, however, through an oval opening corresponding to the palm. The hauberk was also constructed with a hood or coif of mail attached, which could be drawn over the head or flung back over the shoulders.

The conical steel cap with the nose guard, illustrated at the bottom of the page, was the common head-piece of the two previous centuries. The first figure shows the improved head-piece which encloses all the head, except the face, which was defended by a vizor.

PART II

English Costume
of the
Later Middle Ages
The Fourteenth and Fifteenth Centuries

FOREWORD

As in the previous books in this series, my aim has been to select interesting and popular garments, headdresses, footwear, and details of costume of the period. It is not easy in the limited space available to depict the progress of costume during two centuries, and inevitably there are omissions. A great deal of time and thought, however, has been expended on a selection of drawings which will give a maximum of information to the student with limited hours at his disposal and only a slight knowledge of costume.

If the costume of a period is, as Mr. James Laver suggests, the mirror of the soul, there are several interesting reflections in the costume of the fourteenth and fifteenth centuries. The contrast between the dress of the noble and that of the labourer is more striking than at any later period in English history, and it indicates the distinction which the feudal system demanded between the powerful baron and the powerless serf. With the gradual decay of this system later in the fourteenth century, class distinction in dress began a slow process of disintegration which ended only in recent times. Changes in costume were few in the early years of the century, but with the achievement of national unity—the complete fusion of the Norman conquerors and the Anglo-Saxon conquered, and the progress of national freedom in the increasing powers of Parliament—English life showed fresh strength and vigour, which is reflected to a remarkable extent in the costume of the latter half of the fourteenth century. Clothes assumed a new importance, and new and exaggerated fashions made great headway. It was with the arrival of Anne of Bohemia in the 'eighties that the most fantastic and exaggerated fashions made their appearance, and from this time onwards until the Puritan influence of the seventeenth century, costume became more and more ornate. The exaggeration of each phase of fashion beyond the point of absurdity seems to have been the aim of every would-be " Elligant " of the fifteenth century.

The new virility and gladness of English life which found utterance in the verse of Chaucer and his *Tales of the Canterbury Pilgrim* seem to have died with him, but in the century which followed, in spite of the wars with France and the Wars of the Roses, the gay progress of costume continued, and both men and women found ample opportunity for self-expression in dress. Costumes were still fantastic and exaggerated when the acquisition of wealth and material prosperity under the Tudors permitted still further elaboration, so that the fifteenth century closes and the age of Elizabeth opens with pageantry more lavish than at any other period in the history of English costume.

I. B.

*Color Plates for
Parts I, II, and III*

1250
FRONTISPIECE (PART I)

900–1000
(FACING PAGE 10)

900–1000
(FACING PAGE 18)

1000–1100
(FACING PAGE 30)

1100–1200
(FACING PAGE 38)

1100–1200
(FACING PAGE 48)

1100–1200
(FACING PAGE 58)

1200–1300
(FACING PAGE 66)

1300
FRONTISPIECE (PART II)

1325–1350
(FACING PAGE 102)

1375–1400
(FACING PAGE 116)

1400–1420
(FACING PAGE 124)

1420–1440
(FACING PAGE 134)

1440–1460
(FACING PAGE 146)

1460–1480
(FACING PAGE 156)

1480–1500
(FACING PAGE 166)

1520
FRONTISPIECE (PART III)

1500–1510
(FACING PAGE 182)

1510–1520
(FACING PAGE 190)

1540–1550
(FACING PAGE 212)

1550–1560
(FACING PAGE 220)

1560–1570
(FACING PAGE 228)

1580–1590
(FACING PAGE 244)

1590–1600
(FACING PAGE 252)

English Costume
of the Later Middle Ages

1300

1300—1325

CLOTHES worn during the first quarter of the fourteenth century were a motley of a dozen countries. It was a time when England sought and found inspiration for costumes, manners, and furnishings from the Continent and from the East.

It is impossible at this early date to talk of fashion, as we understand the word. Cloth was both expensive and enduring, and one well-woven garment might serve three generations, its usefulness not diminishing with age. Elementary ideas of personal and domestic cleanliness prevailed, and there was a constant struggle against famine and disease. The wars with Scotland and France, and the strife between the Crown and the Barony, left little time for the consideration of dress apart from its utility.

This tendency to severe utility is well illustrated by the two costumes in the frontispiece. These simple loosely-fitting garments, almost devoid of ornament, are typical of thousands that might have been seen in the early years of the fourteenth century.

There is so little change in clothes, and so little variety, in the early period of this century, that one page of sketches is almost enough to show the foundation of practically every type of garment. A man of nobility and wealth wore furs and velvets, and his gowns were usually voluminous and all-enveloping. The women wore a tight-fitting garment, which we will call a kirtle to distinguish it from the outer gown, and over it a surcoat. This garment was split at the sides, and, being sleeveless, displayed the sleeves of the undergarment. A girdle or belt, with pouch attached, was worn either at the waist or a little lower, but little attention was paid to finishing touches. Aprons were worn to a great extent by the people; with this exception, the costume illustrated might be that of a lady of quality. The jester at this time was an important personage in every large household. Later in the century his traditional dress became much more elaborate.

1 3 0 0 — 1 3 2 5 (*continued*)

The coif, a close-fitting bonnet tied under the chin, which enclosed the hair and ears, was worn extensively by men; over this the hat or bonnet was worn. The heads of both men and women inclined to drapery rather than to any formality in headdress. Men wore their hair long—almost to the shoulders. Women always parted their hair in the centre, and wore it in plaits doubled over the ears or confined in a chignon or net. The nets were often ornamented with beads or gilt spangles. In some contemporary drawings the hair is shown in a loose plait or twist hanging down the back.

As the hood, with its gorget and liripipe, became the foundation for dozens of head-arrangements throughout the fourteenth century and the first half of the fifteenth century, it is perhaps advisable, at this stage, to explain how this fantastic fashion began. At first the hood was merely a cowl with a point at the back, with a gorget hanging down over the shoulders. In the next stage the point at the back of the hood was elongated, often to an absurd length, by the addition of a long pipe of the material, or a " liripipe," as it was called. The lengthening of this appendage and the ornamentation of the edge of the gorget were seized on with delight and elaborated to ridiculous extremes by the dandies of the period.

In the early years of the fourteenth century the opening in the hood, which had been previously left for the face, was placed on the head, and the gorget then fell like a scarf from the side or the top of the head, on to one shoulder, and the liripipe on to the other. Later, the liripipe was wound round the head, and the gorget with its jagged edges stood out like a cockscomb. The front part of the facial opening was rolled back to form a brim, and during the fifteenth century this was stiffened, and the liripipe became a wide scarf which was often draped round the chin. The slow evolution of headgear from a simple cowl to the absurdly fantastic head-dresses of the fifteenth century can be traced with ease in the following pages.

1325—1350

THE two costumes illustrated here, of about 1340, have assumed a definite cut and shape which previously had been lacking in both men's and women's attire. The figure-fitting garments are much more attractive than the somewhat shapeless clothes that had been prevalent during the early Middle Ages. The clinging lines were often achieved at this time by lacing down the back, from the neck to the waist.

The working-classes were still wearing the less restricting garments, tied loosely at the waist with a leather girdle, instead of the ornate and wonderfully jewelled belts worn by the wealthy.

The two figures here represented have been taken from the tombs erected to the memory of two of Edward III's children, both of whom died in infancy. That of the boy shows us one of the very few examples of men's civil attire, as obviously the little boy was too young to be represented in armour. The elaborately dagged cloak, with its square enamelled buttons, the high collar, the golden circlet, and pointed bejewelled shoes, all show an advanced stage in fashions for this date, although it is, of course, possible that the tomb was not erected until several years after the deaths of the children.

The golden net on the head of the little princess is interesting as an early example of the emphasis of ornament in front of the ears. The long clinging lines of her cotehardie and the tight-buttoned sleeves are the earliest examples of a fashion which was to last a century or more.

I 3 2 5 — I 3 5 O (*continued*)

Few indeed are the references to clothes in the contemporary records of this time, although we find that the Scots, a wild and somewhat conservative race regarding clothes, took exception to what they considered effeminacy in the attire of their English enemies. Notices were pinned up on church doors about the fashions and manners of the English. One at St. Peter's, Stangate, was as follows :

> " Long beards heartleffe,
> Painted hoods witleffe,
> Gay coats graceleffe
> Makes England thriftleffe ! "

The long beards must have been a fleeting fashion, as there seems to be a scarcity of beards, either long or short, between 1330 and 1350. Painted hoods and hats were worn from about 1325, and embroidered and hand-painted materials were popular throughout the century. The " gay coats " referred to were in all probability the parti-coloured garments, a fashion which survived, in hose at least, until the time of the Tudors.

The costume of a man of the time consisted of the following garments. Firstly the shirt, an undergarment and rarely visible ; over this was worn the doublet, or gipon, as it was then called. The gipon was a closely-fitting tunic reaching to the knees, and its tightly-fitting sleeves were usually visible under the cotehardie, or external garment. The hose were separate, like the stockings of to-day, and were tied to the gipon with a multitude of strings. Hoods were worn by practically everyone ; sometimes they were attached to cloaks, but more often were a separate garment confining the head and shoulders, with a circular aperture for the face.

1 3 2 5—1 3 5 0 (*continued*)

It was towards the middle of the century that English life began to recover some of its animation. Commerce and extended trade in woollen manufacture helped to enrich a nation impoverished and spiritless after a succession of long and costly wars. Prosperity had an immediate effect on costume. The somewhat meaningless draperies of the early fourteenth century took on the clinging lines associated with the costume of the Middle Ages, and dignity and grace appeared where only utility and economy had found a place.

Patterns, though simple in design, were often woven into the materials, and richly ornamented girdles and belts were worn by both men and women. Buttons of fantastic design played an important part in the decoration of gowns and cotehardies, and tassels and cords appeared on cloaks. In fact, the whole order of attire gradually took on more importance and interest.

It was during the 'thirties that the " dagged " fashion first became so popular. The term " dagged " or " jagged " means the cutting away of the edges of garments to form a pattern. Sometimes scalloped or pointed, the fashion offered great scope for individual feelings and requirements, and it soon spread to other garments, even appearing on the tops of boots and shoes. Excellent examples of " dagged " garments may be seen on the figures on contemporary tombs, although it is unfortunate that practically all the men of the period chose to have their effigies representing them in full armour. However, there are a few of children and youths and many of ladies that show, perhaps better than any other records, what beautiful lines appeared in the long dagged sleeves, and the graceful fullness of cloaks and gowns.

1 3 2 5 — 1 3 5 0 *(continued)*

The wimple was worn throughout the century, and the barbette, or band under the chin, which might be attached to the plaits at the side of the face or draped right round the face, was to be seen until the 'seventies. The veil and circlet, or crown, are typical of the fourteenth century. No woman's head was dressed without a veil of some description, either draped round her chin or worn over her head, or both. A gilded or jewelled circlet or an ornate net was also worn. Head-dresses constituted almost the only extravagance permitted to women at this period. While crowns or circlets were worn by the wives and daughters of noblemen, veils, nets, barbettes, and hoods were worn by all.

Women's clothes at this time fitted the figure closely to the hips and then splayed out into a wealth of graceful folds. The kirtle or under-gown was very tight-fitting, with sleeves buttoned from wrist to elbow. The surcoat worn over this was sometimes cut away at the sides in order to display a jewelled hip-belt. Occasionally the surcoat had sleeves to the elbow, and a tippet was worn. The tippet in this case was a band of contrasting material or fur, varying in length from a few inches to several feet, sewn round the arm, and allowed to hang from the elbow.

So scarce are the records of this time that, with the exception of the Loutrell Psalter and the Queen Mary Psalter, almost the only examples of English wearing apparel are to be found on tombs and wall-paintings. It is a great loss to students of contemporary fourteenth-century decoration to find that a number of valuable sources have been defaced or removed during the last hundred and fifty years. There are a few books printed at the beginning of last century which give tantalising glimpses of figures on tombs which no longer exist. Unfortunately these sketches are hardly sufficient as a basis for reliable detail.

1 3 2 5—1 3 5 0 *(continued)*

It is interesting to note that in the year 1339 Edward III received thirty thousand pounds from duties levied on the exportation of wool. The king's hold on Flanders at this time was largely due to the fact that, had this exportation ceased, half the population of the large Flemish towns would have been unemployed. Shortly after he invited Flemish weavers to take up their residence in England, and looms were set up in the eastern counties, especially Kent, and from the middle of the fourteenth century onwards woollen fabrics were woven in England.

The wealthy continued to wear silk and velvet and cloth of gold imported from abroad, but the less affluent welcomed the new woollen materials with joy and delight.

The figures on the opposite page are as typical as any of this particular twenty-five years. The hood and dagged gorget worn by the man were seen in hundreds of slightly different variations during this period, and so were the tight-sleeved kirtle, and button and tippet-trimmed surcoat worn by the woman. The veil, loosely worn over the plaited hair, was possibly the simplest method of head-dressing at this time, and certainly very charming. The simple spot pattern on her gown has been taken from a contemporary design, and if not actually woven into the material, was hand-embroidered. Some of the exquisite embroidery on the dresses of this period must have taken half a lifetime to execute, and it is fortunate in this age of leisure that by the time the embroidery was finished the gown was not too old-fashioned to wear.

1350—1375

THE difference between the attire of the ordinary people and that of the nobility was more noticeable in the men's attire than in the women's. The citizen's wife might wear a dress almost identical with one worn in the household of a knight, differing only in the apron and probably the wimple worn by the citizen's wife, and the coronet and veil and possibly the cloak worn by the knight's wife.

The vogue for embroidery spread to the homes of all, and many long hours were spent in work of this kind. Bands of simple design were to be seen at the neck and hem, and often on the sleeves, of practically all feminine attire.

The power of the Church at this time seems to have been quite negligible as regards sobriety and modesty in clothes. It is particularly interesting to note this when it is realised that priests and nuns all wore the same attire as their brothers and sisters who had not taken holy orders. The court of Edward III was singularly unhampered by the disapproval of the Church, and the extravagance and vice of the nobility was reflected in their dress.

A contemporary writer, disgusted by a recent exhibition at a tournament, gives a good description of the fashionable male attire worn during the 'sixties: " Whenever there was a tournament there came a great concourse of ladies of the most costly and beautiful, but not of the best in the kingdom, sometimes forty or fifty in number, as if they were a part of the tournament, in diverse and wonderful male apparel, in parti-coloured tunics, with short caps and bands wound round their head, and girdles bound with gold and silver, and daggers in pouches across their body . . ."

1350—1375 *(continued)*

Although it was not until the 'eighties that William Langland wrote the *Complaint of Piers Plowman,* the social conditions which he so vividly describes were very much the same as in the 'seventies, and the contrast between the poor working man and the wealthy churchman was as great.

His description of the ploughman shows how pitiful and poverty-stricken was his condition :

" His cote was of a cloute, that cary was y-called,
His hood was full of holes, and his hair oute,
With his knopped schon (shoes) clouted full thykke . . .
His hosen overhangen his hokschynes, on each side . . ."

He also speaks of the friars wearing spotless linen underneath their outer garments, which were so dirty that corn might be grown in them ! The cotton cope which covered them was only an outward sign of endurance, for beneath this they were well-padded with short fur or beaver coats, and socks were surreptitiously worn inside the shoes to keep their feet from chilblains. Piers Plowman's bitterness is further increased by the fact that the clergy asking for alms in the street were often the proud possessors of six or even seven copes, and could afford the luxury of red shoes.

It was at about this time that regulations for moderation in the garments of the Grey Friars were issued : " Bredth of hood not wider than the shoulder bone, length of gown not longer than its wearer, bredth not more than sixteen spans, nor less than thirteen. The sleeves over the joint of the finger and no furthur. The mantles must be of vile and coarse cloth not curiusly made or pynched about the neck."

1375—1400

THE closing quarter of the century held the greatest changes in costume. With the marriage of Richard II and Anne of Bohemia in 1383 the court became a centre of luxury, and the royal couple were leaders of the exaggerated fashions which prevailed. Anne brought with her a variety of previously unknown ideas regarding clothes, the most important being the gigantic and ornate head-dresses, which were worn throughout the following century, increasing in size as the century advanced.

It was a period of fantastic costume, the beginning of the ornate and decorative attire that is always associated with the Middle Ages. The houppelande, a gown made in a bell shape, with a hole for the neck in the centre of the circle, made its appearance during the 'eighties. This was worn by both men and women, and was cut in varying lengths to suit the wearer. The feminine edition was usually cut with a large aperture at the neck, and was held with a wide belt, usually embroidered, which reached from the waist to close under the breasts ; this new high waist was definitely revolutionary, and its popularity almost exceeded that of the surcoat cut away at the sides.

The masculine houppelande was high-necked, often covering the ears. Sometimes the garment only reached the thighs, but often it fell in increasing fullness to the ankles. Houppelandes were worn right through the following century, and the gracefulness of the heavy folds was an outstanding feature of the dress of the Middle Ages. At a later date the folds were sewn in to the waist, giving the skirt a more formal effect.

The man's hood on the opposite page is of the separate type, which was not as popular as those which enveloped the face and shoulders. His surcoat is the houppelande with the now popular bell-shaped sleeves. This type of sleeve, turned back and lined with contrasting material, and allowing the sleeves of the doublet beneath to be seen, remained in fashion throughout the following century. The jewelled girdle not only encircles the waist, but it also holds together the front of the skirts. The shoes are typical of perhaps a few years earlier ; the fashion of embroidering and bejewelling went out with the arrival of the exaggerated long-toed shoes. The girl's dress is definitely earlier than the arrival of Anne of Bohemia, probably about 1380.

1 3 7 5 — 1 4 0 0 (*continued*)

Chaucer gives an excellent description of the houppe-lande in his picture of the friar :

> " Of double worsted was his semi-cope,
> That round was, as a belle, out of the presse."

There are many allusions to clothes in the history of this period—partly because of the new importance attached to them by the court, and partly because the people found in them an excellent opportunity for pointing a finger at the extravagance of their oppressors.   John Ball, " a mad priest of Kent," as Froissart calls him, protested strongly at the wilful waste and unbridled extravagances of the rich : " They are clothed in velvets and rich stuffs, ornamented with ermine and other rich furs, while we are forced to wear poor cloth."   Another interesting note is that Wat Tyler bought sixty doublets for his men at the amazingly low price of thirty marks, and incidentally never paid for them !

It was during the 'eighties that women first rode side-saddle ; previously they had all ridden astride like men, with their skirts tucked into a bag-like affair.

The toes of shoes became even more exaggerated in length than before ; the points were often tied to the knees with gold or silver chains to avoid the possibility of the wearer tripping over them.

A wealth of colourful description is to be found in Chaucer's *Canterbury Tales*.   His brilliant portrayal of the numerous pilgrims leaves little to the imagination as to their appearance. Perhaps the most curious thing to us about all these descriptions is the importance placed upon the pouches, knives, and jewellery ; these etceteras obviously played a very important part in the attire of the well-dressed.

1 3 7 5—1 4 0 0 (*continued*)

We read that the Wife of Bath wore scarlet hose, that the Merchant wore a " Flaundrish bever hat," and that the young Squire wore his hair curled and

" Embroidered was he, as it were a mead
All ful of fresshe flowers, white and red."

The ' Mellere' wore a " Whit cote and a blew hood " ; we read of the ' Reeve ' that :

" His beard was shave as nigh as ever he can,
His heer was by his eres round i-shorn.
His top was dockèd lyk a priest biforn.
Ful longe were his legges, and ful lene,
Al like a staff, ther was no calf y-sene.

.   .   .   .   .   .

A long surcote of blew uppon he hadde,
And by his side he bar a rusty blade."

A long description of hairdressing is given in the picture of the Pardoner :

" This pardoner had heer as yellow as wex,
But smothe it hung, his lokkes that he hadde,
And therwith he his shuldres overspredde.
Full thinne it lay, in lengthes, one by one,
And hood, for jolitte, werèd he none,
For it was trussèd up in his wallet.
He thought he rode al of the newe set,
Disheveled, save his cappe, he rode all bare."

The Sergent of Lawe " rode but hoomly in a medly cote, Girt with a girdle of silk, with barres smale ! " And the Doctor of Phisik

"In blue he clad was al and sangwyn
Lynèd with taffeta and silke thin."

1 3 7 5 — 1 4 0 0 (*continued*)

There is no doubt that the works of Chaucer are, from the costume point of view, unrivalled in valuable detail. With the possible exception of some of the Diaries of the seventeenth century, no other contemporary source of any period provides us with such a wealth of interesting and valuable data as to modes and manners of the times. Not only does Chaucer describe the general appearance of his characters, but he gives also minute descriptions of materials, colours, and fashions in jewellery and hairdressing, and other interesting details which the more staid chroniclers of history fail to record.

References to some of the more exaggerated clothes of the period are to be found in several of John Wyclif's tracts. The wealthy churchmen, who paraded themselves in exaggerated sleeves, costly materials, and curled hair, was no light matter, and the delicious humour to be found in the writings of his contemporary find no place in Wyclif's writings. Little escaped Chaucer's quick eye, and he records all the minor points of detail in the Monk's costume :

> " I saw his sleves rounded at the hand
> With fur, and that the fynest in the land.
> And for to fastne his hood under his chyn
> He hadde of gold y-wrought a curious pyn :
> A love-knotte in the gretter ende ther was."

The number of references to jewellery made by Chaucer indicates what an important part it played in the costume of the period. Even the nun had her share of personal adornment :

> " Ful faire was her robe, as I was war.
> Of smal corál aboute her arme she bare
> A paire of bedes, the greatest were of grene ;
> And theron hung a broch of gold ful shene,
> On which was first i-writ a crownèd A,
> And after, *Amor vincit omnia.*"

1400—1420

THE manuscripts, both illuminated and illustrated, of this century, show a wealth of beautiful detail in both colour and line, but unfortunately there was no one to take Chaucer's place, and descriptions of costume are sadly lacking. As many of the manuscripts took twenty years or more to execute, it is difficult to estimate with any strict exactitude the date of the costumes illustrated, although a number of minor, if not major, changes in style over a period of twenty years help to decide within ten years or so the date of the dress.

It should be remembered, too, that the fashions at court changed slowly, and took a long time to filter down to the country, and that the garments had a long life ; thus it is possible to realise why a particular gown may be almost identical with one of fifty or sixty years earlier.

The most obviously new innovation of this period was the short doublet. The hose had been cut to reach the waist, possibly as much as fifteen or twenty years earlier, and gradually the skirts of the outer garment became more and more brief, until they were eventually merely a pleated frill some six inches below the waist.

The houppelande in its most exaggerated forms, with sleeves almost as full as the gown itself sweeping the ground, was a favoured garment for those wishing to appear more dignified and prosperous than those who favoured the absurdly abbreviated tunics. Two so entirely dissimilar fashions have rarely appeared together in the history of costume.

I 4 0 0 — I 4 2 0 (*continued*)

Variety and exaggeration in dress seem to have been general tendencies at this time; she who could outdo her neighbour in the size of head-dress and the width of skirts would deem the effort well worth while. The young squire of the day spent his all on the latest thing in embroidered surcoats and painted hoods, and went to great pains that his hair should at least be as well curled as his neighbour's. According to the miniatures of the period the hair was often crimped, giving the effect of having been tightly plaited and then undone. It is possible, however, that this was the contemporary interpretation of curly hair, and that all the young squire did was to plait his locks tightly overnight. Chaucer's Squyer, " with lokkes curled as if they lay in presse," rather gives us this impression.

Several new styles of sleeve made their appearance at the beginning of the fifteenth century. Where previously only the tight-fitting and the bell-shaped, or a combination of the two, had been worn, there were now sleeves of practically every known shape and size. The new bagpipe sleeve, made like a gigantic bag, fitting at the shoulder and hanging in loose folds to be gathered into a tight band at the wrist, was popular for a few years. Two examples of this may be seen on the opposite page, that at the bottom being a very subdued version. The surcoat was often worn with a sleeve to the elbow, and an example of the tippet worn at the wrist of the gipon may be seen on the last figure on the page.

The tight sleeve with a roll or gathered puff at the shoulder was worn more often with the short-skirted garment. All sorts of varieties in the arrangement of the bell-shaped sleeve were to be seen; sometimes the sleeve was turned back to the elbow, showing a fur lining; sometimes it was gathered into a bunch at the shoulder and left to fall in deep folds under the arm. Some sleeves were so excessively long and full that the lower parts were tied in great knots to save them dragging along the ground.

I 4 0 0—I 4 2 0 (*continued*)

Few indeed were the garments worn at this time that were not either embroidered or patterned in some manner or other ; even when plain cloth was used it was decorated with bands of embroidery or fur. The passion for decorating even extended to the tops of hose. Tapestry-like embroideries were seen on almost every woman's gown. Embroidery had ceased to be merely a matter of spot patterns ; most of the designs were large, and were often repeated only two or three times on a garment. The designs seem to have been arranged after the garments were made, as often the central floral or imaginative motif appears on the front of a gown, with the rest of the design merely emphasising it. In smaller designs the motif appears symmetrically on the shoulders and in the middle of the back.

When spot patterns were used, they were usually larger and more dignified than those in vogue during the previous century, but their popularity waned as the century proceeded, and they made way for the boldness and exaggeration which was characteristic not only of design. Indeed, boldness and exaggeration, combined with a sense of dignity, typifies the outlook on costume during the greater part of the fifteenth century. Hardly a single fashion was introduced that was not carried to one extreme or another after it had been in vogue for a few years.

Literature had fallen to a very low level ; Chaucer was dead, and there was no one to record for posterity the life and work of the time; indeed, almost the only literary productions were pamphlets and rhyme-sheets, and translations of French romances, which appeared in large numbers. From the point of view of costume they are quite useless, and if it were not for the letters of the Paston family it would be difficult to bridge the gap. Their letters are invaluable, and contain many details and descriptions of costumes and materials in use between 1420 and 1500.

I 4 0 0—I 4 2 0 (*continued*)

Head-dresses were already tall and ornate, but they became more and more exaggerated. The head-dress assumed more importance, and in order that nothing should distract attention from it, it became the fashion to pluck the hair on the forehead and on the back of the neck. It was a common sight to see ladies of fashion plucking their necks in public with the aid of a small mirror or a piece of polished metal. It was not considered any more remarkable than it is now for a woman to be seen powdering her nose or adding a touch of lipstick in a 'bus or drawing-room.

The illustration opposite shows the horned head-dress, completely covered with a veil. The simple lines of the dress are an excellent background for the amazing quantity of fur lavished on the immense sleeves. It is interesting to note that the man is wearing chains attached below the knee, to which the toes of his shoes may be tied. His short gown has the bagpipe sleeves already mentioned, and a " harness " is slung across the shoulder. Often these " harnesses " had bells attached. In the manuscript from which this costume is taken the gown is white, with a bold green and pink design ; the hat scarlet, with a gold coronet. The habit of wearing a crown on the hat was practised a great deal by royalty and the nobility.

I 4 0 0—I 4 2 0 (*continued*)

By 1420 the gipon was made with the high collar, and the surcoat was cut low at the neck to reveal the contrasting colour of the collar beneath. Usually the outer gown had the neck cut in a V-shape behind, and was edged with fur.

Large beaver hats, and those made of velvet and cloth, were almost as much worn as the hood, which by this time differed a great deal from its original form. The cockscomb effect was more frequently seen than previously, and the liripipe had now assumed the title of tippet. A " tippet " at this time seems to have been the name used for practically all pieces of material that were depended from the main garment.

The steeple head-dresses assumed a gigantic height during the 'twenties and 'thirties ; the veil was elongated, and was often worn over the arm to prevent it trailing the ground. It was about this time that the rather attractive eye-veil was added to this type of head-dress. The head-dress like a flower-pot on the opposite page, worn with a veil under the chin and a tie at the top, was not seen later than the 'forties. It was not nearly so popular as the steeple, horned or rolled head-dresses, examples of which are seen from the end of the fourteenth to the end of the fifteenth centuries.

It is interesting to compare the simplicity of the woman's bonnet or hood at the bottom of the page with the complicated head-dresses worn at this time. It appears to be made from a perfectly straight piece of material folded in half and sewn down the back only, the front part being cut and turned back at the face.

1420—1440

THE extravagant use of furs throughout the fifteenth century gives the impression that England was rich in animals. Much fur was imported, but it was obviously too expensive to be used profusely except by the wealthy ; the others had to content themselves with home-cured fur.

The man's gown on the page facing is cut at the sides, front, and back to facilitate riding, and is obviously lined with fur throughout. The lady's gown is richly trimmed with ermine ; the tippets on her sleeves are exaggerated into a double-skinned and voluminous drapery hanging from a band at the elbow, the end narrowing so that it may be tied round the wrist should it prove too heavy or cumbersome. It will be noticed that the box-like head attire is surmounted by a circlet of an irregular diamond shape. These circlets were also worn on top of the horned head-dress.

Shoes with extremely exaggerated toes were not so popular as they had been a few years earlier. The fashion of attaching chains to the toes of the shoes, mentioned a few pages earlier, had proved to be unsatisfactory. It was quite impracticable, and when people found it was difficult for them to walk a few steps, and impossible to walk upstairs, the craze soon died out.

The taste for fantastic clothing spread to people of all classes, which so little pleased the nobility that laws were introduced restricting those with an income of less than forty pounds a year from indulging in the most extravagant fashions. Gowns and jackets had to cover the buttocks, and the pikes on shoes were to be no longer than two feet in length !

1 4 2 0—1 4 4 0 (*continued*)

Men, as well as women, wore elaborate headgear, and their immense hats were exaggerated and ornamented to an absurd extent. The fashion for decorating the crowns of hats was first indulged in soon after the middle of the fourteenth century, but a more orthodox brim than that shown on the opposite page was then worn. Gigantic soft-crowned hats, like an electric bulb in shape, another like a three-tiered turban, and numerous other queer and exaggerated shapes, are to be seen in contemporary illustrations.

Indeed, there seems to be no limit to the variety of head-dresses termed fashionable. Fringes for men were very popular at this time ; the hair was still curled and worn long, although it was often cut in a fringe all round, slanting up from the nape of the neck at the back, covering the tops of the ears at the sides, and merely an inch or so less in length on the forehead. It is curious that at a period when women tucked their hair out of sight, plucked their eyebrows, and sometimes, if we are to believe contemporary portraits, cut their eyelashes, that men should wear their hair frizzed and curled, and in elaborate fringes.

Tall, soft leather boots were worn for riding, either reaching well up the thighs or only half-way up the shins. In both cases they were turned back at the top and were often lined with a contrasting colour. Spurs were always used for riding, even on shoes and soled hose.

Although the illustrations on the opposite page do not show a variety of patterned materials, practically everything was richly embroidered, usually with large and somewhat irregular designs.

I 4 2 0—I 4 4 O (*continued*)

The costumes depicted on the opposite page have all been specially selected to show the more sober and less exaggerated costumes worn by the older and more dignified people of the age. With the exception of the large bold designs on the materials they have little in common with the extravagant attire of the fashionable. Their somewhat sombre simplicity is in sharp contrast to the youthful and flippant garments illustrated on the previous page.

The central figure at the top of the page shows the more sober version of the horned head-dress. The horns are merely padded points over the ears, and are used as a support for the veil, which is trimmed with gathered or rouched material. Heavy gathered rouching was very fashionable for trimming, and was to be seen on even the most sober garments. Fur of all kinds was lavishly used, both for gowns and hats, and often the complete hat would be made of fur.

Small children at this time rarely wore more than a short tunic, unless they were fully clothed as miniature men and women for some very special occasion. Many examples, however, are to be seen of the very youthful page clad in an abbreviated X-shaped tunic, his long shapely legs in hose, his hair well crimped, and with a short, almost invisible, fringe peeping from beneath his flower-pot hat.

The central figure at the bottom of the page shows the method employed to fasten the hose to the gipon, when as often happened the hose were not cut to reach the waist.

The shoes illustrated are of the more useful type, some resembling a modern bedroom slipper, others consisting of a sole of leather sewn on to the hose itself.

I 4 2 O—I 4 4 O (*continued*)

By the 'thirties head-dresses had assumed gigantic and
imposing proportions.   Many of these amazing con-
ceptions can be seen on the figures on contemporary
tombs, where a detailed and relief study will reveal far more
than any sketch can possibly show.   Both this and the
colour drawing on page 147 are based on the same idea.
This example, with the addition of horns beneath the coronet,
makes it one of the most weird and wonderful head adornments of the time.

The surcoat worn by this lady has the sides cut away
until merely a small strip of fur-edged material supports the
skirt.   The dark kirtle worn beneath is made almost skin-
fitting in its tightness.

Both these figures show the lavishness of the extremes
of fashion at this time.   The man, with his curled hair,
huge beaver hat, laced doublet, bunched shoulders and striped
hose, was the gallant or fop of his period.   Men's waists
appear so small in contemporary portraits that one wonders
if any form of corset was worn.   Undoubtedly belts were
worn much too tight to be comfortable, to give the X-shape
effect which fashion demanded in the fifteenth century.

Extravagance and exaggeration are terms which occur
frequently in describing the costumes of this period, and if
a detailed study of social life was within the scope of this
book references to greed, lust, and selfishness would appear
with equal frequency in this age, when religion meant little
and sorcery and magic were believed in by all.   When one
of the punishments for women guilty of immoral behaviour
was for their hair to be cut off to the ears, and it was scan-
dalous for women to show an inch of leg beneath their
cumbersome skirts, and the Countess of Cobham did penance
for practising magic, it is not difficult to imagine why Joan
of Arc was condemned as a witch and a sorceress.

1 4 2 0—1 4 4 0 (*continued*)

Fantastic headgear was at its height, both literally and figuratively, during the 'thirties and 'forties of the fifteenth century. There are so many types and varieties of absurdly exaggerated hats, especially those worn by the men, that one page of drawings is quite inadequate to give even a representative selection. As the less fantastic fashions must have a place in this book if it is to be of any use as a general guide to the dress of the time, several of the more modest types of hoods, hats, and other head adornments have been included in the two following pages of drawings.

The large beaver and velvet hats, the dagged or jagged gorget, and tippet, and the nightcap or coif at the bottom of the page, are three examples of the more sober forms of headgear. Headwear as an expression of personality is perhaps a limited study in these days of mass production, but in this period of the Middle Ages students of psychology would find more than enough material for study. There seemed to be hats for every mood—fantastic or frivolous, sober or learned, and every man could let himself go in creating a model more exaggerated, more ornate, and more complicated in design than that of his neighbour. For a few years at least the men refused to be outdone by the women in the matter of head-dress ; even the originally simple hood was exaggerated out of all recognition, the tippet, now wide and embroidered, often trailed the ground, the gorget fell in a profusion of ornamented folds over the shoulders, and the roll or brim assumed a stiffened and enlarged appearance.

I 4 2 0—I 4 4 0 (*continued*)

The rolled head-dresses worn by the women at this time might take practically any shape. Instead of merely forming a frame for the face, as it did at first, it was now a joined affair, making a padded circle of any size to suit the wearer. Sometimes they were like a lifebelt in shape, and worn without a veil; sometimes the pad was exaggerated to a couple of yards in circumference, and bent into a variety of shapes. Heart-shapes and U-shapes were particularly popular. The front part was usually worn low on the forehead, and the sides lifted to show the fretted nets over the ears. As these rolls were often arranged eighteen inches or so above the head, it was fortunate that the architecture of the time allowed for this exaggerated height of headgear, and that the low beams of a few years later had not yet appeared.

The knobs on the head-dress of this period are particularly absurd, and it seems that if a head-dress was not considered sufficiently fantastic to please its owner, the addition of a knob on the top made amends for any other deficiency in the imagination of the wearer, if not in the eye of the beholder.

The influence of the East is very noticeable in the turban-like head-dresses worn by both men and women. The advancements and refinements of Eastern civilization were being gradually introduced to the West, and almost every European country imported silks and rugs, and exquisite pieces of workmanship, to grace the halls of the wealthy and to adorn their noble personages. The beautiful and exotic colours of the materials had a great and lasting effect on the costumes and decorations of the period to follow.

1440—1460

IN the year 1440 there is an interesting letter written by
Agnes Paston to her husband, asking him to do some
purchasing for her and her sister. " . . . Yil ye woulde
byen her a goune, here moder Yeve ther to a godely furre.
The goune nedyth for to be had ; and of colour it woulde
be a godely blew, or erlys a bryghte sangueyn. I prey you
do byen for me ij pypys of gold." In modern English this
means that her sister wanted a gown well-trimmed with
fur, either blue or bright red, and that she herself would be
obliged if he would buy her two reels of gold thread for
embroideries.

Colours and materials at this time were of the richest,
and most brilliant ; velvets, damasks, figured satins, linen,
keyrse, blanket musterdevelys, tisshew, cloth of gold, and
cloth of silver, camlet, morey, frieze taffeta, and broadcloth,
were materials most worn. Musterdevelys was a greyish
soft woollen cloth, and was worn until about the middle
of the sixteenth century ; camlet was a heavy cloth made of
camel's-hair, and exceedingly expensive.

Cloth of gold was not to be worn by any one lower than
a lord's estate ; neither was the use of sable permitted to
any one without a title. These restrictions and others previously mentioned limiting the luxuries of dress and the
extremes of fashion to certain classes seem to have been
disregarded in many cases. We find, for instance, mention
of two gowns of cloth of gold in the wardrobe of Sir John
Falstolf in 1459.

It was during the 'forties and 'fifties of the fifteenth century
that costumes reached the peak of exaggeration.

1440—1460 (*continued*)

A wealth of description of clothing is to be found in the Will of Sir John Falstolf. It is impossible to include all the details, and space can only be found for some of the more interesting data :

" First, a gown of cloth of gold, with side sleeves surplis wise.

Item 1. Another gown of cloth of gold, with straight sleeves and lined with black cloth.

Item. Half a gown of red velvet.

Item. Gown of blue velvet upon velvet long furred with martyns and trimmed of same, sleeves single.

Item. Red gown of Lord Cornwall's livery, lined.

Item. Gown cloth of green 3 yards.

Item. Side scarlet gowns not lined.

Item. Chammer cloak (one cut in the centre) of blue satin, trimmed with black silk."

Among his numerous jackets we find one : " The brest and slevs of blak felwett, and the remnant of russet fustian."

Some of the detailed descriptions of the hoods are extremely interesting : " Hode of blakke velvet, with a typpet half damask half velvet y-jagged." Another : " Hode of depe grene velvet, jagged upon the rolle," and another was " of russet velvet, with a typpet half of the same and half blew velvet, lined with blew damask."

There is yet another of purple velvet without roll or tippet. The tippet in this case referred to the appendage which had once been the liripipe and now hung from the roll in a profusion of folds.

The " Items " mentioned above are only a small proportion of the garments described in the Will. This gentleman owned doublets, petticoats (skirts), jackets, gowns, hoods, etc., in profusion, mostly in velvets and other rich stuffs.

I 4 4 0—I 4 6 0 (*continued*)

It will be noticed that from time to time one of the pages in each group of costumes is mainly devoted to the less exaggerated costumes of the period, and the page facing illustrates the more sober fashions of the time. It is not easy to maintain a sense of proportion ; the extremes and extravagances more readily attract the eye, and contemporary sources usually give only the more exaggerated interpretations of costume and neglect the less spectacular garments of the period.

The huge bell sleeve turned back at the wrist and showing the tight under-sleeve was worn by all classes. The figure of the boy at the bottom of the page shows an example of the detached sleeve tied at the shoulder with " points," and not attached to the gown under the arm. The sleeve of the gipon underneath is slit up to the shoulder and tied in a number of points, revealing the shirt-sleeve beneath.

The fashion for " points," a string similar to a boot-lace, was first introduced in about the 'fifties of this century. These " points " were means of tying a slashed garment where it would best display the garment worn beneath. They became even more popular in the reign of Henry VIII, and were then seen on practically every item of male attire.

It will be noticed that the examples of dress on the opposite page have little in common with those on the previous page, where an attempt has been made to indicate the elaborate decorations of fur, embroidery, and trimming on every garment. Even the veils worn on head-dresses had spangles or rouching, or ornaments of some kind, and nothing that could be decorated seemed to escape the ever-busy needles of the ladies of quality.

1440—1460 (*continued*)

In the year 1449 Margaret Paston writes to her husband, asking him to buy her some cloth, " That ye wille do byen sume frese to in maken of your child is gwnys; ye shall have best chepe and best choyse of Hayis wyf, as it is told me. And that ye wyll bye a yerd of brode clothe of blac for an hode fore me of 44d or 33d or 4 shillings a yerd for there is no good fryse in this town."

Shopping must have been a sorry business for ladies of the time. There were few shops to be found outside the big cities, and to a large extent everyone relied on pedlars. These travelling salesmen could only carry a limited stock, and if they had nothing suitable, materials for a new gown or hood had to be purchased through the services of a relative staying or living in London.

Some time in 1445 William Paston writes to his wife, asking her if she could buy some materials for his liveries. Her reply indicates how limited were the stocks kept in the smaller towns. She writes, " As touching for your liveries, there can none be got here of that colour that ye would have of, neither murrey, nor blue, nor good russets, underneath 3 shillings a yard at the lowest price, and yet is there not enough of one cloth and colour to serve you."

1 4 4 0—1 4 6 0 (*continued*)

Referring again to the invaluable Paston letters, there is a complete inventory three years later of the gowns owned by Clement Paston while at Cambridge, including " A short green gown, and a short musterdeuyllers gown. A short blue gown, a long russet gown trimmed with bever, and a long murry gown." Fur was still used a great deal, and the furs most frequently used seem to be ermine, beaver, marten, bogey, and sable.

The monstrous winged head-dress did not appear until the middle of the fifteenth century. It must have a great deal of care in laundering, and as starch was unknown at this period, some difficulty must have risen in stiffening it. Probably a solution of glue or size was used. The fashion did not last so long as the still popular steeple and roll, and comparatively few examples are to be found, although one portrait of Elizabeth Woodville shows an almost obliterated version of this butterfly effect.

1460—1480

THE charming gown worn by the lady on the opposite
page is of an unusual design ; the scalloped bodice
and the richly embroidered skirts being of different materials.
The design on the skirt is taken from a contemporary
miniature. Several of these bold and beautiful designs have
been the inspiration for some of the modern designs found
on woollen embroideries and furnishing materials sold in
most of the big London shops to-day.

The long gown worn by the man has an amusing
method of adornment in the three long thin cords hanging from the yoke of the gown. They were almost invisible, and although weighted with beads, they must have
got constantly tangled, and altogether been an incredible
nuisance. But comfort seems to have been a secondary
consideration in this century, and few garments permitted
the freedom we demand to-day.

It was during the 'sixties that the fashion for short cloaks
for men became prevalent. They were cut in varying lengths
to reach the hem of the doublet, whether the doublet reached
only the waist or continued half-way down the thighs.
One or two examples of this fashion are to be found on the
following pages, including a very extreme example on page
73, which barely reaches the waist. It is quite obvious that
this gentleman had an income of more than forty pounds
a year !

1 4 6 0—1 4 8 0 (*continued*)

The two short gowns or jackets worn by the men at the top of the page are interesting examples of new designs. The first is worn without a belt or girdle, this being unnecessary as the pleats are sewn down tightly to the waist at the back. The doublet in this case is lower in neck-line than in previous modes. The second gown is almost armour-like in its simplicity ; cut from some stiff material, it is made up without gathers or pleats of any sort, except for the slight gathering at the shoulders, which was a necessary finish to any fashionable garment in the latter part of the fifteenth century.

At the bottom of the page will be seen a new idea in boots. The boot is cut in the usual soft leather, but fits the leg so tightly that there is no drop over at the top ; the tops are cut to form a point at each side, and a design is embroidered round the edge.

A curious version of the horned head-dress appears next to the figure in boots. The hair is drawn through the horns and falls in exaggerated waves through the extreme ends of the tubes. It is extremely unusual for the hair to be seen, as at this time every wisp of hair was tucked out of sight. The sleeves are also unusual, as no less than three garments are visible ; the under-garment with tight-fitting sleeves is the smock or shift.

The use of " points " as a means of decoration can be seen in two of the figures on this page, where they are merely tied to the upper sleeve and serve no useful purpose. The small boy's hose are tied to his abbreviated gipon, and can be seen through his sideless gown. An example of the shoes worn by women can be seen on the first figure. They were made of soft leather, and with little variation were worn throughout the century. Clogs or pattens were worn by all in bad weather, and wooden soles were worn on many shoes.

1 4 6 0—1 4 8 0 (*continued*)

Margery, the young wife of John Paston, was one of a type that has persisted through the centuries. In her letters to her husband during his absence from home there are constant references to the fact that she has " nothing to wear." In one letter she writes asking him to buy her a new gown, adding that " I have no gowne but my blak and my grene," and both of these she is tired of wearing. She also demands a girdle, as she has only one fit to wear, and her friend Elizabeth Peveral has at least fifteen or sixteen. Girdles at this time were very important items in a lady's wardrobe. They were of two main types: the wide ones, which were the only trimming to a simply-cut gown, and a narrower type jewelled and decorated for more elaborate gowns.

Girdles increased in importance and value, and a few years later, in the will of Dame Elizabeth Brown, several of different materials and design are bequeathed to various friends and relatives: " Three embroidered girdles, one tawny silk, with buckle and pendant, another purple, three of purple damask, some of ' tisshew,' some of ' red tisshew gold.' "

In 1471 John Paston writes home for some of his clothes, which he finds he requires: " Two long gowns, and two doublettes, and a jaket of plonket camlet, and a morey bonet out of my cofyr."

It will be noticed that the long gowns were nearly all split at the sides at this time. Formality in their folds was brought almost to the stage of pleats. The effect of bunched shoulders was sometimes obtained by merely catching the folds at regular intervals across the arm-hole, as in the back view at the bottom of the opposite page. The sleeve, with two openings, one at the elbow and one at the bottom of the sleeve, were worn a great deal, and as will be noticed in the coloured drawing on page 167, by slipping his hand through the lower opening the boy has given an entirely different arrangement to the sleeve.

1 4 6 0—1 4 8 0 (*continued*)

Another example of sewn pleats on a gown is to be
seen here. The belt is merely an accessory, and does
not hold the waist-line, as is usually the case. The sleeves
are split right up the inside of the arm and can be worn
either hanging loose, as seen here, or with the hand thrust
through the fur-edged cuff at the bottom.

Soft cloth and velvet caps of absurd shapes were much
worn by all men at this period.

It will be noticed that the steeple head-dresses have, by
this time, assumed lappets reaching down to the shoulders
on each side. This must have been the beginning of the
gable head-dress worn at the beginning of the sixteenth
century, an example of which may be seen on the last page
of the book. The steeple itself was often decorated. A
variety of patterns, of which the diamond one seen here was
most popular, were used to adorn these sugar-loaf head-
dresses.

Deep cuffs of a contrasting material were worn on the
tight-fitting sleeves after the beginning of the 'sixties. Low-
necked gowns were not often seen after this time, and when
the V was cut too low to suit fashion's decree, modesties
filled the gap at the front. This example has an interesting
finish to the neck, as the effect of a collar is achieved without
one being used. No girdle or belt is worn, the gown being
cut to fit the figure closely at the waist. The fashion for
wearing the kirtle pleated and fuller than the gown itself
was carried on into the following century.

1 4 6 0—1 4 8 0 (*continued*)

On the opposite page may be seen the differences in the angle, height, and design of the steeple. The upper example is worn without the eye-veil, but with long exaggerated lappets decorated with jewels, and reaching well over the shoulders. The lower example is more exaggerated in height, and may be considered the extreme of the fashion. As can be seen, the hair is strained off the face, giving the head rather an egg-like appearance.

The back view next to this figure is an example of the butterfly head-dress, and shows how the ends of the material were folded and fastened at the back.

Long quills and feathers were beginning to be worn in men's hats. Pheasants' quills and others of a stiff nature were the most popular at first, but after a few years the softer types of feather took their place. These were draped round the hat or allowed to fall gracefully over the shoulder. From about 1470 until the beginning of the nineteenth century feather-trimmed hats for men never ceased to be popular.

An example of the hood worn in the original manner, but with the liripipe wound round the head and tucked in at the side, may be seen at the bottom of the page. The hood was rarely seen worn after 1465, being forsaken for caps and hats. Beaver, velvet, cloth, and wool were the most popular materials of which they were made. Even the country people preferred caps to the somewhat clumsy hoods which they had been wearing for over twenty years.

The head-dresses of the Middle Ages were gradually subsiding; the horns had gone, the ornate circlets had vanished, and soon women's head-dresses were to be referred to as " bonnets." To our modern ears this term seems quite unsuitable for the still cumbersome and ornate head-dresses.

1480—1500

THE will of Dame Elizabeth Brown, referred to a few pages back, includes several details of dresses which show us how popular and important were gowns trimmed with fur. Indeed, there seem to be few garments at this time which were not either trimmed or lined with fur of one sort of another : " Violet gown furred martons, black furred with grey, black furred white, black furred martons, a kirtle of tawny chamlet, and a purfil of ermine two skins deep." The will also includes a piece of cloth of gold with dropis.

A purfil was the border or trimming at the bottom of the gown. These were obviously made separately from the gown, and attached to any gown or kirtle as required.

The sleeves of the boy's gown on the page facing have already been referred to. He is wearing one sleeve loose, and he is seen putting his hand through the cuff of fur at the bottom of the other.

The cap and hood is worn hanging down the back, with the tippet over the shoulder to keep it in place. This was frequently worn purely as an ornament, and another hat, quite separate, was worn on the head.

The girdle with the pouch at the side was a very important item of every man's attire. These pouches were almost always decorated with embroideries, beads, or painting of some sort. The long-toed shoes were not so popular as they had been throughout the earlier part of the century. They were now made almost fitting the foot, with a point an inch or so in length. The round-toed shoe was to be the fashionable shape for a few years before the arrival of the absurd square-shaped shoe of the early sixteenth century.

1 4 8 0—1 5 0 0 (*continued*)

Although history tells us that at this period the
nobles were sorely over-taxed to fill the coffers of
Henry VII, the pageantry of exotic and costly gowns and
garments, of a richness and extravagance hardly rivalled by
the court of Elizabeth, seems to belie this. The use of gilt
and silver and the lavish use of superb and wonderful furs
by the nobility and wealthy merchants hardly indicates that
they were taxed to the extent of impoverishment.

The visit of the Venetian ambassador to England at
the end of the century is recorded. His impressions of the
country are flattering, and some of his comments on the
manners and modes of the late fifteenth century amusing.
" They all from time. immemorial wear very fine clothes,
and are extremely polite in their language. " Among other
things, he is amazed to find that men take off their hats in
the street as a salutation to each other.

Amongst the newer fashions are the striped and plain
hose. The fashion for parti-coloured hose and for striped
hose had been in vogue for many years, but the combination
of one striped and the other plain was not introduced until
about 1490. The man's short gown at the bottom of the
page is cut away in front, revealing the pleated front of the
doublet beneath. The different sleeves on this page will be
noticed ; the one at the top on the right is lengthy, and
though not nearly so full as those worn earlier, is considerably longer. The absurd little hats worn by the men
at this time are in sharp contrast to the gigantic hoods
worn a few years earlier.

Men wore their hair longer at this period, often allowing
their curls to reach half-way down the back.

1 4 8 0—1 5 0 0 (*continued*)

It will be noticed that the outline of women's costume underwent a drastic change during the last few years of the fifteenth century. Fantastic head-dresses were no more, and the long flowing lines of the gowns of the Middle Ages gave place to the high-waisted bodices and gathered skirts of the early Tudors. The kirtle became a more important garment ; and it was often made of a richer material than the gown itself, and showed several inches below the outer skirt.

The formal drapery of the head was the beginning of the coif, which became so popular during the thirty years of the following century. But perhaps the most noticeable change in women's attire was the sleeve. For so many years the tight-fitting sleeve had been regarded as a necessary foundation for another, that the new idea of wearing a comparatively loose-fitting sleeve, revealing the wrist and sometimes the lower part of the arm, must have been readily welcomed.

One last bequest of the Paston family shows the use of at least one cosmetic—face-powder. In the year 1482, Margaret Paston leaves a purple girdle harnessed with silver and gilt to her daughter Anne. A powder box, a coarse girdle of blue harnessed with silver and gilt, and beads of silver enamelled. Also to her servant, Agnes Swan, she leaves her muster-develys gown furred with black, and a girdle of black harnessed with silver and gilt and enamelled.

The references to the ornamental belts give the impression that in the last part of the fifteenth century, at any rate, they were for the most part composed of gilt or silver, and enamelled in rich colours, rather than bejewelled.

1 4 8 0—1 5 0 0 (*continued*)

The method of ornamentation used on the sleeves of the gown worn by the man on the page facing is extremely interesting. The pattern has been cut at the edges instead of being split, which was the usual manner of displaying the shirt sleeve beneath. The points of the pattern are tied with " points " at two places. The fur-trimmed cap, the long feathers, and the long hair are all interesting innovations.

The woman's cap, with the ears enclosed in a net and a ring on the forehead, strikes a new note when accompanied by long curls at the back, and only a small black cap, instead of a gigantic one as worn a few years earlier. The simplicity of her gown still holds something of an earlier period, and the collar and cuffs and the gathered skirt show slight indications of the fashions to come.

The clothes worn during the time of the House of York show a startling difference to those worn under the Tudors, due not to the personal endeavours of Henry VII, who had little leisure for the contemplation of fashion, but to the beginnings of the intellectual revolution of the Renaissance. Although there is little to choose between the ornateness and exaggeration of both periods, the change in general outline is remarkable. The long sweeping lines of the ladies' gowns have nothing in common with the full-skirted bunchiness of the early Tudors. The square clumsy outline of the time of Henry VIII has little in common with the somewhat effeminate fussiness of the short-skirted, long-legged, be-curled gentlemen of the previous pages. Although the clothes of the fifteenth century are perhaps less enriched with costly jewels and enamels than those worn during the sixteenth century, the wonderful colours and furs are more than recompense.

1 4 8 0—1 5 0 0 (*continued*)

The century closes with gorgeous pageantry. Lords and ladies arrayed in cloth of gold and ermine, with girdles of exquisite and intricate design, and decked with priceless furs and jewels, and gold and silver chains worth a king's ransom, make this period more lavish than any other in the history of English Costume.

The incredibly lovely materials, with years of work in their sight-destroying embroideries, and the wonderful examples of hand-weaving, are so dignified in their design that they make the costly materials worn a century later almost vulgar in comparison. Designs of imaginary floral figures, bold and overpowering though they were, were far more effective than the tiny naturalistic interpretations worn during the time of Elizabeth.

This last page of head-dresses shows the fusing of the old and new. The gable as it was first worn is shown ; and another example was worn by widows who still clung to the wimple as a sign of mourning. The steeple at last went out of fashion the year 1490. One or two of the ornate head-dresses of the fifteenth century were still to be seen after that date, but mostly the simpler coif and veil was favoured. Hair was to be seen once more for a few short years after a century of hiding. The small cap and long curls worn by the men show a striking contrast to the ornate, overpowering, and truly absurd erections worn on the cropped heads of fifty years earlier.

Some of the most ridiculous fashions ever worn in this country appear in this century, but they are more than balanced by some of the most charming and dignified garments ever designed to enhance the beauty of the human form.

PART III

English Costume
in the
Age of Elizabeth
The Sixteenth Century

FOREWORD

ALTHOUGH this book bears the title " The Age of Elizabeth," it actually covers the entire sixteenth century. To show the evolution and slow, steady development of costume it is necessary to go back to structural beginnings : the trunk-hose, the flat wool caps, and numerous other equally interesting details of dress in Elizabethan England—all had their origin in the Courts of Henry VII and Henry VIII.

Elizabeth's reign was a magnificent pageantry of exotic and fantastic costume, unrivalled in our history, which had its inspiration in the glamour of her father's Court, and owed its ultimate execution to the influx of riches into a country impoverished by recent royal extravagances. There was a notable increase in the refinements of domestic life, and with the coming of panelled rooms, latticed windows, and carpeted floors, an altogether higher degree of personal fastidiousness was displayed. Not only was more attention paid to dress, but cosmetics were introduced from the Indies, and so were several new and exciting perfumes ; both these innovations tended to give a more cultivated finish to an exotic costume.

Competition, always an important factor in the history of costume, became a potent impulse, capable of greater gratification than ever before in this age when Englishmen were first journeying beyond the sea in search of commerce or adventure. A new skirt from Spain, a new hat from Italy, a hat-band from France, a slashed bombasted doublet from Germany—all were possessions to be coveted. And so it was throughout the century, each man vying with his neighbour for the possession of the greatest number and variety of enviable articles of adornment.

It is clearly impossible to illustrate here more than a small fraction of the designs that may be found in contemporary manuscripts, wall-paintings, portraits, miniatures, effigies, and actual garments still surviving. Equally impracticable would be any complete description of the minute and myriad methods of ornamentation which, in this period of most complex costume, adorned practically every item of apparel from hat to shoes. I have aimed, therefore, to condense and simplify, so that in these few hundred drawings may be found representative and typical examples of the garments which in all probability were the daily wear of our predecessors some four centuries ago.

I. B.

1520

1500—1510

WHEN the sixteenth century opened, the wealthy were spending vast sums on clothes. At the wedding of Prince Arthur and Catharine of Aragon in 1501 the Duke of Buckingham wore " a gowne wrought of needle worke and set upon cloth of tissue, furr'd with sables, the which gowne was valued at £1500. Sir Nicholas Vause, knight, wore a gowne of purple velvet dight with pieces of gold, so thick and massie that it was valued in golde besides the silke and fur a thousand pounde. Very wonderful it was to behold the riches of apparel worn that day, with puissant chaines of gold, of which two were specially noted, to wit: Sir T. Brandon, knight, master of the king's horse, which wore a chain valued at 1400 pound, and the other, W. de Rivers, esquire, master of the kinges haukes, which chain was valued at a thousand pound." And it should be realized that money then possessed quite four times its value to-day.

Men's clothes were not only costly but so rich in their variety that it is now barely possible to distinguish all their pieces as individual garments. So numerous were the additions of sleeves, skirts, fronts, and other spare parts that we cannot state definitely of what the complete costume consisted. The body-garment, however, may be assumed to have been five separate pieces. First, the shirt; here at least we are safe, for the shirt was the foundation garment and always had sleeves. It was made of holland, cambric, or lawn, and frequently it was embroidered. The neck-line was low and showed the collar-bone, occasionally so low that it scarcely covered the shoulders; more often it was round than square in cut. The sleeves were full and loose to the wrist, where they were finished with a tiny band or frill.

Over the shirt was worn the doublet, which may or may not have had sleeves. Sometimes, too, the sleeves were separate pieces tied at the shoulders with points, and showed the shirt underneath through the gaps. The doublet was usually padded and rarely reached below the waist during the first ten years of the century. Next came the jerkin or coat, similar in cut to the doublet, though it usually had sleeves of some sort, either long or to the elbow. Sometimes it was skirted, or the skirts might be entirely separate affairs, in which case they were termed *basses*.

1500—1510 (*continued*)

A gown, or more rarely a cloak, was worn over the jerkin. Usually made of some heavy woollen material and lined with fur, this could touch the ground or barely reach to the knee, as pleased its owner. Finally, men wore from the waist to the foot an entire garment—tights, hose, or stocks. These, as you may see, were simple and tight-fitting at the beginning of the century. A tendency to adorn the upper part with slashing and embroidery was the first sign of the eventual trunk-hose, predominant throughout the period. By about 1510 upper-stocks had definitely assumed the aspect of separate breeches, although actually this was not the case. These were made of cloth or velvet, cut on the cross of the material to give the necessary elasticity and stretch ; knitted hose were not introduced till much later in the century.

Shoes were flat-soled, like a mule without a heel, though occasionally an inch or so of leather was added as a covering for the heel. Boots of soft coloured leather were worn for riding.

Occasionally we see examples of "rush" shoes, made of plaited straw or reeds, and worn by the peasantry. These were worn over the entire foot, and the loose ends of rush formed a rough fringe around the ankle. This type of footgear seems to have been worn extensively on the Continent, and the paintings of Hans Holbein the elder show us numerous varieties. Clogs also were not unknown on this side of the Channel.

1500—1510 (*continued*)

Women's dress, although by our modern standards distinctly complicated, was actually exceedingly simple, except in rare cases when the slashing actually cut the gown into separate parts.

First was worn the shift, similar in cut to the man's shirt ; then one or two petticoats, the upper one often pleated and of a contrasting colour to the gown ; then the gown itself, with full trailing skirts. In some instances the train was lifted and fastened to the girdle at the back, to show the lining, and to facilitate walking. The gown was either laced at the back or fastened in front. The neck was square and low in front, and V or U shaped at the back. Its sleeves were usually bell-shaped, with the lower edge turned back several inches to form immense cuffs which revealed the lining and displayed the sleeves underneath, which were attached to the elbow or shoulder. Plain, full sleeves, tight at the wrist, were still very popular, and there are numerous examples of tied and slashed sleeves. Also the entirely separate sleeve, tied in four or five points at the shoulder and showing the puffed shift through the gaps, was frequently worn.

Belts and girdles were a necessary part of dress for both sexes. The men had a pouch or purse hung from one side with a slit behind to hold the dagger ; this fashion, however, was superseded almost at the beginning of the century by a separate sheath and dagger attached to the right-hand side of the belt. The woman's girdle was made of cord or chain, and from it hung a miscellaneous collection of household requisites, anything, in fact, from keys to a book.

Clothes were slashed, embroidered, furred, and guarded— that is, having wide bands of velvet (usually black) or embroidery sewn on the garment as a form of decoration. Precious stones, gold and silver chains and clasps, and numerous rings were worn extensively. Gloves, when worn, were cut at the knuckles to show the rings beneath.

1500—1510 (*continued*)

Male headgear might be described under two categories :
the *biretta*, and the beret, very similar to that worn to-day
but with a brim, usually turned up and cut in one or more
places to make flaps, which frequently overlapped. Women's
head-dress was less simple. The Dutch *coif*, or cap, was
worn quite frequently in England. This consisted of one
tight-fitting cap over the front of the head, with the hair
piled up in a great coil behind it, and over this the actual
coif, usually made of embroidered lawn. Young unmarried
girls frequently wore their hair loose, or tied with a " snood,"
or tucked into a gold net after the French style. While the
definite English tendency was for the *coif* and veil, its popularity was challenged about 1503 by the gable head-dress,
which lasted with modifications for forty years or more.
The gable head-dress was the roof-like arrangement worn
by the second figure on the preceding page. This particular
example shows the earliest type with the long side-pieces,
which later were folded back across the top of the " gable."
The front edge was always decorated with precious stones,
and the lappets at the sides were profusely embroidered.
At first the veil at the back hung down over the hair, which
was loose ; but later, as we shall see, the veil was split and
folded back over one side of the head-dress. In the latter
instances the hair seems to have been piled up under the
head-dress behind, as few of these examples show us the long
hair hanging down at the back.

1510—1520

FOUR hundred years ago there were no middle-classes as we know them to-day. One was either a peasant, " one of the people," or else one belonged to the nobility, which included wealthy landowners and merchants. The working people's clothes were of necessity far simpler in cut and material than those worn by their employers, and we may safely assume that for the first half of the century there was little or no change in the apparel of either men or women among the peasants.

The men wore simply a shirt and tights, the latter of cloth reaching from waist to toe, covered by a belted doublet of some rough woollen material that finished an inch or two above the knee and had long sleeves. Their boots or shoes were usually made of leather and covered the ankle. Sometimes a cloak or gown was worn for extra warmth, and the flat cap, with a brim, similar to those already described, was seen everywhere.

Peasant women wore simple woollen garments, their shifts frequently made of linsey-woolsey. The gown itself (seen in the upper drawing on p.195) was cut with a tight bodice, sometimes laced in the front, fairly close-fitting sleeves, and a full, short skirt barely reaching to the ankles. A large apron of holland or some coarser fabric was always worn, and the belt or girdle served to carry any small article that the housewife might require from time to time. The *coif* or cap was worn throughout the period, with modifications. Women's hose were of cloth and reached just above the knee, where they were tied; shoes were of the loose slipper variety with a flat sole and round toes, and occasionally wooden shoes were worn in muddy localities.

About 1518 the " split " sleeve came into vogue for ladies of fashion. As may be seen in the costume illustrated here, the sides are caught together with gold clasps instead of the more usual " points." This mode remained in favour practically throughout the century.

1 5 1 0—1 5 2 0 (*continued*)

England at this period was the sole manufacturer of woollen stuffs ; therefore wool, frieze, rugge, broadcloth, kersey, and similar materials were worn extensively by all classes, although the poor frequently wove their own home-spun. Only the wealthy could afford such sumptuous fabrics as cloth of gold or silver, velvet, satin, tissue, tinsel, and fine damask, which were all imported at fabulous prices from France, Spain, and Italy. About 1515 a definite German tendency prevailed in England : heavy pleating and excessive slashing are noticeable on most garments, jerkins being so closely pleated as to consist almost entirely of three layers of material. Both the jerkin and gown assumed a yoke or collar similar at the back to a sailor-collar, and to this were attached the folded edges of the pleats, leaving the fold itself free and standing out from the garment instead of sewn flat as in the modern method of pleating. Such a gown is worn by the man on the left at the bottom of the page opposite. Sleeves became more and more excessive, longer and looser. Some were cut at the elbow or shoulder to allow them to hang loose, or to be tucked into the belt or girdle at the side and display the sleeve of the doublet or jerkin worn underneath.

Striped tights or hose, still worn a great deal on the Continent, were also frequently seen in England, but the mode of stocks with legs made from different coloured materials was seldom adopted on this side of the Channel.

Men's hair was still worn long, though usually cut in the manner of a longish " bob " in preference to the shoulder-length curls seen at the opening of the century.

1510—1520 (*continued*)

While a number of varied examples of women's apparel naturally appear in these pages, it should be understood that the nun-like head-dress and gown were still the most generally worn. The lady in black on the opposite page is, perhaps, the most typical Englishwoman. The rather exaggerated figure at the top right-hand corner is more representative of the Flemish or German style often seen in England at this time. The extravagant modes of slashing and tying with " points " were general in most European countries.

The unfortunate children of the sixteenth century were dressed as exact replicas of their parents, but this does not seem to have hindered them from playing such games as hoops, leap-frog, stool ball, and many others equally active. Babies were all swaddled or swathed until they reached the age of six months or more, the idea being that the legs and arms must necessarily grow straight if tied in that position. There is small wonder that infant mortality was so excessive ; the heat inside these swathings must have been unbearable during the summer months, and should the mother or nurse bind them too tight, the miserable child was doomed to deformity of the shoulders and thorax.

1510—1520 (*continued*)

The woman on the right at the bottom of the preceding page is wearing the gable head-dress with its lappets folded back to show the long side-pieces of the coif worn underneath. Hairdressing with this form of head-dress now assumes a mode of its own: either the hair was parted in the centre and the front part bound with ribbon and recrossed on the forehead, or—perhaps when the hair was thin or short—the front hair was encased in rolls of striped silk or cotton and arranged in a similar manner. The hair at the back was worn loose under the veil. Occasionally we find examples of the striped pad pushed farther back on the head and showing the centre parting of the hair in front, as may be seen among the group of heads on page 203.

The large velvet hats, slashed and decorated with gems and feathers, were not of English origin, but were brought over from Germany, France, and Spain. Several leading English ladies of the Court favoured these more masculine fashions. Anne Boleyn was rarely painted in anything nun-like, but her known portraits represent quite a valuable collection of rather masculine hats. The coif and the circlet of gold and gems with a short veil behind appeared about 1503, and seem to have remained in favour until supplanted by the Tudor cap made so popular by Mary Queen of Scots.

1520—1530

A NOTICEABLE change in the cut of the under-garment occurred about the 'twenties of this century. The neck-line gradually rose until it took the form of a minute frill—the first small beginning of the ruff to come. This fashion was more general for the man, women still preferring an open neck in most cases, although there are many examples of the high-necked shift.

Heavily embroidered materials gained brilliance by the addition of sewn pearls and beads and other semi-precious and precious stones. In the frontispiece is shown the first example of the treble sleeve, a fashion rigidly adhered to whenever the bell-shaped sleeve to the gown was worn. This consisted of a detachable short sleeve or cuff of a stiff embroidered material—in its early stages frequently striped ; worn over the lawn or cambric under-garment, and joined by "points," thus showing the under-sleeve, which was pulled out in puffs. This large cuff finished a few inches above the elbow, and, as the fashion progressed, became larger, until it formed a complete half-circle of stiff material folded and fastened in the manner described.

About 1525 the woman's skirt, which previously had been a complete affair, was cut up the front to form an inverted V, which disclosed a sumptuous embroidered petticoat, usually of contrasting colours to the gown or kirtle. A tendency to stiffen the petticoats and make the skirt stand away from the body was first noticeable about this date. The train also had practically disappeared from general use by about 1520, although it was still worn by ladies of the Court and for all ceremonious occasions ; the train of this period was not the separate hanging train as we know it to-day, but the trailing point which was a feature of all gowns worn during the first twenty years of the sixteenth century.

The figure on the left at the bottom of the opposite page is an exceedingly interesting example of German fashions, a striking contrast to the very English lady facing her. There are few remaining examples of such pleated skirts, probably the weight of them was too much for the majority of women to bear, and the mode could not have existed for more than a very few years. It is, however amusing to note the amazing similarity between this figure and those of fashion plates of about one hundred years ago, between 1825–30. Fashions are for ever changing—but never advancing.

1520—1530 (continued)

Of trunk-hose, the breeches are called "upper-stocks," and "nether-stocks" is the name for the stocking-like part covering the foot, calf, and frequently the thigh. Practically throughout the century these were joined together to form one complete garment. The second man on the previous page is wearing one of the earliest pairs of "paned" upper-stocks, an effect achieved by slashing in even strips, or more rarely by means of separate ribbon-like attachments of embroidery. It will be noticed that as the century advanced they became looser and were stuffed out to their fullest capacity. This same man is also ornamented with *picadils*, the folded and cut material visible on the shoulders, wrists, and where the upper and nether stocks are joined. This exceedingly popular form of decoration was used by both sexes, and several examples, especially as a shoulder and neck decoration, will be found in the ensuing pages.

Shoes, which previously had been somewhat round-toed, developed into the well-known square, padded, and slashed shape in which Henry VIII was wont to be depicted. Sometimes these were ridiculously exaggerated, even to eight or nine inches width at the toe, with tufts of coloured lining pulled out through the slashes. They were tied at the ankle with a thin leather lace, which came from behind the heel of the shoe, not from the instep. On the page facing is an example of loose *panes* tied just above the knee to form yet a second bulge. At this early period, however, little or no stuffing was worn, merely a loose lining which could be drawn out through the panes if the wearer so desired.

1 5 2 0 — 1 5 3 0 (*continued*)

With the rise of the neck of the doublet and jerkin a small collar sometimes appeared, though this fashion seems to have been more military than civil until about 1535, when it became general.

The head-dresses illustrated here need little or no explanation. The gable at the bottom has the lappets folded and the veil split and laid back over the head-dress. The man next to this is wearing an exaggerated form of the traditional cap, and the loose, open pleats on his gown are clearly seen. The top left-hand figure is taken from a portrait of Anne Boleyn, and the gewgaw that hangs from the ridiculous cap is a typical addition.

It is impossible to over-emphasize the general extravagance of ornament among the wealthy. The amazing richness of embroidery, and the dazzling addition of jewels, could not conceivably be illustrated in a much larger book than this. If it be borne in mind that practically every square inch of the garments reproduced in these pages was ornamented, slashed, embroidered, and bejewelled, that magnificent pearls, jewels, and precious stones adorned practically every finger, trimmed every head-dress, decorated every neck, and were woven into every garment, then it may be possible to gain some idea of the extravagant splendour of a Court in the reign of Henry VIII. At no later period in the history of our country has the Court wallowed in so much gold and silver and priceless materials. And probably at no time have the poor been so squalidly housed and filthily garbed as they were during this amazing reign.

1530—1540

THE female example on the facing page is not, strictly speaking, the most typical of the period 1530–1540. It is, indeed, the German type of gown and hat adopted in England during the 'thirties, and rarely seen later than 1534. However, I have chosen it in this instance to give the reader some idea of the detail in design which I have already mentioned. Spot patterns and interchange designs were very popular, and the acanthus leaf figured extensively in all floral designs. The lady's gown or kirtle is of purple velvet, richly worked with silver thread; the lower part of the sleeve is white cloth-of-tissue with a traced design in gold. Under this she wears a pleated petticoat of yellow damask. The neck of the gown is heavily set with stones, and her belt and necklet are both of gold, with rubies and pearls inset. Her hat is of black velvet, also bravely adorned with many precious stones.

The gentleman beside her is a typical example of the fashionable Englishman of the late 'thirties. From now on a new item of men's clothing takes shape in the form of a waistcoat. The doublet is cut low to reveal the splendour of this beautifully embroidered and pearled garment. The latter in its turn is slashed to show off the fine lawn or satin shirt beneath. In this example the sleeves are made of the same material and design as the waistcoat, the doublet being sleeveless. The doublet is made of black velvet and decorated with bands of crewel-work, as is the skirt or base, which is split in front, showing the cod-piece, a feature of men's apparel until the 'eighties. The stocks are made of velvet, black at the top, and blue nether-stocks. Over all is the jerkin of light blue broadcloth lined with miniver; the elbow-length sleeves are slashed and show the fur linings.

1530—1540 (*continued*)

Let us for a moment imagine ourselves transported in time over just four hundred years back to the scenes of Anne Boleyn's coronation. From the Tower to the Temple the city is alive with excitement. Cheapside, Cornhill, and Grace Street are marvellously decorated with gold and silver cloth and rich velvet hangings. The constables of the City, richly clad in velvet and silk, hold great staves in their hands to keep back the seething crowd of would-be spectators. From every gaily-trapped window excited and curious heads crane to get a glimpse of the new Queen.

Amid yells of applause and welcoming cheers the procession winds its way through the narrow, overcrowded streets. Foremost rides the Lord Mayor, splendid in his crimson velvet gown lined and trimmed with fur, his large gold chain flashing impressively in the sunlight. He is followed by footmen in white and red damask, then by twelve mounted Frenchmen clothed in blue velvet with blue and yellow sleeves, their horses' trappings a blue sarsenet ground with white crosses. Then proceeds a stately assortment of Knights, Squires, Judges, Gentlemen, Abbots, Barons, Bishops, Earls, and Marquises, these all gowned in scarlet or crimson. The Knights Commanders of the Bath wear gorgeous violet velvet, with hoods embroidered in gold and silver and " purled " with miniver !

Then at last, as we grow dizzy with so brilliant a spectacle, the Queen appears, a striking figure in white amongst such a riot of colour. Her litter of white cloth of gold is borne by two palfries in white damask. Her kirtle is of white cloth of tissue, her mantle of the same, wonderfully furred with ermine ; down her back hangs her fair hair, and on her head is a coif with a circlet about it full of rich and rare stones. And carried by four knights is the canopy of cloth of gold with gilt staves to shield her from the sun.

1 5 3 0—1 5 4 0 (*continued*)

Behind the Queen ride the Lord Chancellor and the Masters of the Horse; then come the ladies of the Court, all in scarlet velvet turned up with gold and tissue, their horses in magnificent trappings of cloth-of-gold. And, last of all, the gentlewomen of the Court are drawn in chariots of cloth-of-gold and clothed in scarlet and crimson. The procession passes, and a motley collection of shopkeepers, marketers, children, beggars, and sightseers crowd across the road, cheering. Such is the indelible picture that is left us by a contemporary historian. There are a thousand and one equally interesting details, especially of the feast: the amazing dishes they ate, the incredible quantity of wines and ales consumed, how Anne sat at the head of an immense table—her ladies to the left, gentlemen to the right—and was served with twenty-six dishes to each course.

This page of drawings and the one preceding it give various examples of the gradually changing style; the high neck for the shirt was practically always worn, and was finished with a *partlet strip*, or upstanding separate collar, which perhaps was the first version of the starched atrocity worn by men of to-day. A tiny shoulder-cape of velvet or cloth was often worn by ladies at this time, and a high-necked yoke of some material contrasting in colour with the gown seems to have been very popular until the 'fifties. Skirts were gradually becoming fuller and fuller, the hems just touching the ground all round.

I 5 3 0—I 5 4 0 *(continued)*

Several different types of caps were worn indoors by matrons and by domestics, and many varieties of the coif developed eventually into the upstanding semicircular head-dress, of which the top right-hand illustration is an example. This was so heavy with jewels and ornaments that it had to be tied under the chin with a narrow white cord to stop it sliding down the back of the wearer's head.

From about 1535 men's caps began to be worn with the brim down, instead of turned up as had previously been the case. The same style of cap was adopted by many ladies and worn over the coif. Between the years 1530 and 1540 a short bowl-like cut of the hair was introduced for men— a transition stage between the " bob " and the short hair fashionable for half a century from about 1545 ; an instance of this style appears on the next page, worn by the boy in blue. Ear-pieces, cut to cover the ears and nape of the neck, were apparently quite a regular addition to many caps, both for men and women. Sometimes a close velvet cap with ear-flaps and a cord under the chin was worn, this seems to have been called a " night cap," though whether it was worn day and night is impossible to say.

1540—1550

HERE is an example of the bell-skirt without folds, cut across the weave of the material to give the skirt the flared effect at the hem. In its earliest stages it is doubtful whether any actual wire structure was worn; the full, creaseless effect was probably obtained by padding at the hip and by a stiffened hem, combined with the addition of numerous petticoats. However, with the introduction of the Spanish *vertingale* about fifteen or twenty years later, there appears little or no difference in the outline except, perhaps, for an added width of hem.

There was a general tendency to tightness of contour about 1540. The sleeves, for instance, previously soft and malleable, became stiff and somewhat bulky, owing to a certain extent to the increased embroidery on the surface of the materials, and also to the craze for bombasting or stiffening which was just beginning to be noticeable. High leather corsets were generally worn by ladies of fashion, and these were responsible for the curious bolster-like effect so evident in Holbein's portraits.

A dress with a yoke nearly always seems to have had a high stand-up collar open in front. There are also a few examples of the yoked dress finishing with a minute ruff. In the example opposite the yoke is made of fur, but instances of this are rare.

The bonnet-like cap worn by the small boy is certainly amusing and not wholly devoid of charm; it was apparently worn solely by children and elderly men. The other child has his jerkin guarded with the fashionable narrow black bands.

1540—1550 (*continued*)

It is exceedingly difficult to find contemporary examples of the costume of serving men and women of this period—no doubt few, if any, ever had the opportunity of sitting for their portraits. An excellent example, however, is reproduced in each of the drawings opposite. The woman's dress is particularly interesting, and shows us that pleated petticoats were in general use; the little striped cap is of an unusual shape, in fact I have been unable to find more than three or four similar examples, and one of these was made of fur. The idea of fastening the skirt to the belt was probably to protect it from getting unnecessarily spotted in front, for although the effect obtained is in itself exceedingly becoming, it is doubtful whether such was the chief consideration.

Two interesting points to note in the male figure at the top are, firstly, the *mock coat*, a cloak with sleeves entirely for ornamentation; and, secondly, the upper stocks or breeches which, as is typical in these garments' early stages, have a tight-fitting hip-yoke, the *panes* only beginning from the top of the leg, and reaching half-way down the thigh. In this instance they are joined slantwise. The huge square shoulders, padded and bombasted, reached their height of absurdity during this decade, and slowly sank back to a more normal form. At the close of Henry VIII's reign (he died in 1547) shoes began to be made with leather or velvet, covering the instep, and with an inch or so of added protection for the heel. The toes, still squarish, were less exaggerated, and slashing was made in some instances both sideways and upwards. With the death of the King fashions seemed suddenly to mark time, and until the accession of Elizabeth in 1558 very little change took place.

1540—1550 (*continued*)

Bodices or stomachers of gowns gradually assumed a point in front, in preference to the straight line at the waist. About 1545, and for some five years later, they were fastened down the front, the opening being faced with jewels or embroidery and stiffened with wooden busks.

Little girls were forcibly corsetted at a ridiculously early age, and quite probably this was the cause of the deformed shoulders of so many women mentioned by contemporary historians, both at this date and later in the century. It certainly seems impossible, to our modern minds, that any child's bones could develop in a normal manner when hampered with corsets which not only reached from armpits to hips, but were made of leather, wood, or even metal. But these ancestors of ours must have been amazingly hardy. They lived and died surrounded by such an odd mixture of revolting cruelty, dirt, and disease on the one hand, and on the other sumptuous wealth, splendour, and bravery seemingly out of all perspective. Their streets were so foul with drainage and rubbish that clogs, or *chopins*, had to be worn to lift their feet above the filth. Yet their damp and draughty halls were decorated with priceless tapestries, furnished with wonderful hand-carved furniture, and hung with beautiful damasks ; their tables were set with gold and silver cups and platters, and their kitchens richly and plentifully supplied with every conceivable variety of meat, fish, and fowl.

1540—1550 (*continued*)

These sixteenth-century Englishmen were compounded of paradox. They could apparently witness, merely as interested spectators, an acquaintance being hanged, drawn, and quartered. They could set out in small ships to discover new worlds and face unknown dangers. And yet they were terrified of witchcraft, and wore charms and amulets to avert the evil eye, and consulted oracles, and indulged in love-potions in all seriousness. They grumbled and worried over the problem of traffic-control in the City, and over the price of meat when it rose from three-farthings a pound to one penny. At times they were so strangely like ourselves, and at times such worlds apart. Their persons reflected these extremes, especially in the lack of fastidiousness beneath gorgeous exteriors. Baths were considered unnecessary and unhealthy, fresh air was bad for the lungs, sweet scents were held by most to be evil—cloying the senses and there-fore inviting the devil. Small wonder that when Henry walked abroad he carried in his hand " an Orange whereof the substance had been taken out and filled up with a sponge full of vinegar and other confections against the Pestilent Ayres, the which he most commonly held to his nose in a press."

Men's caps became gradually larger in the crown until crown and brim were almost the same width ; the crown was higher, too, than formerly, and somewhat stiffer. About 1550, ruffles came into being. At first, however, they were devoid of starch, which was not discovered until some ten years later ; they were made of holland or lawn and, as will be seen in the illustration, somewhat irregular in form. The tiny ruffle at the top of the *partlet* strip was quite general for both sexes.

1550—1560

DURING this decade the people of England were under three successive sovereigns, each totally different in character and qualities, and their changing influences reacted noticeably upon the style and cut of clothes, even if there was no great variety in costume until after Mary's death.

The first three years, under the youthful Edward VI, saw little or no change. The boy was delicate, and the country seemed to stand still, waiting to see what would happen next. But with the accession of Mary, and the introduction of a Spanish prince as king, fashions began to change. Various Spanish styles were brought into the country, the chief of them the *vertingale*, or farthingale, a somewhat similar affair to the crinoline of the nineteenth century. An amazing variety of new head-dresses and caps supplanted the rather hackneyed coif-and-circlet and the gable head-dress, and for men a hat took the place of the flat cap in many instances. Throughout her reign Mary herself clung tenaciously to the old styles, and innovations were certainly not adopted with any display of interest on her part; the Court, therefore, was practically compelled to adhere to the high-waisted, bell-sleeved gowns, and the coif or caul with the circlet. The caul head-dress with the circlet disappeared at the end of Mary's reign, and probably it was cast aside with a sigh of relief. Most certainly it was exceedingly awkward and heavy to carry, and we read of Mary's coronation that " she wore . . . on her head a caule of cloth of tinsel beset with pearl and stone, and above the same a round circlet of gold beset so richly with precious stones that the value thereof was infinite. The same caule and circlet being so massive and ponderous that she was fayne to bear up her head with her hand." She must have had a ghastly headache after the twelve-hour ceremony.

1550—1560 (*continued*)

In the year 1556 the Ambassador of the Emperor of Russia came to England to pay his respects to Mary and Philip, and there is an interesting list of the gifts showered upon him to take back to the Emperor, which reflects the amazing value set on fine raiment :

" First, two rich pieces of cloth of tissue.
Item, one fine piece of scarlet.
Item, one fine violet in graine.
Item, one azure cloth.
Item, a notable paire of brigandine, with a murian covered with crimson velvet, and gilt nails."

A personal gift to the Ambassador from the Queen included :

" One rich piece of cloth of tissue, a piece of cloth of gold, another piece of cloth of golde raised with crimson velvet, a piece of crimson velvet in graine, a piece of damask purpled, a piece of purple velvet and a piece of crimson damask."

So overjoyed with this wonderful gift was the Emperor that he promptly returned the compliment by having large quantities of rare furs and live animals shipped to the Queen of England. History unfortunately does not state whether these fine beasts were immediately slaughtered for their magnificent fur, or if they were kept as royal pets.

The five years of Mary's reign were among the cruelest and most cold-blooded in our history, yet we find details of these polite international exchanges of pieces of cloth described at far greater length than any of the epoch-making slaughters or executions, possibly because the latter were too numerous and commonplace to be commented upon.

1550—1560 (*continued*)

The bell-shaped sleeve totally disappeared with the accession of Elizabeth in 1558. The new style favoured a tight-fitting sleeve with a large "puff" at the shoulder and a tiny frill or ruffle at the wrist. This puff was frequently quite separate, or it might belong to the gown and the sleeve itself be separate. The new arrangement was equally popular for men's wear. The full bombasted and slashed sleeves never quite lost favour throughout this reign; about the year 1590, indeed, they became even more popular than at any previous date.

Mantles, or *surcotes*, with short puff sleeves were worn, even indoors at times, their fullness increasing at the hem to give an idea of even folds from top to bottom. Many examples of these delightfully formal garments may be seen upon the effigies on contemporary tombs; but in such instances it is quite impossible, owing to the absurd effect of any but the simplest drapery on a recumbent figure, to obtain any idea of the Spanish *vertingale* or full-bottomed skirt which was undoubtedly worn at that time.

Probably the reason for so many changes in fashion about 1558–1600 was that Elizabeth was a comparatively bright young person, who had been imprisoned and suppressed for many years. The effect of sudden access to practically unlimited wealth and freedom and power was that she promptly stocked her wardrobe with all the gowns she desired. We certainly know that she was fond of clothes—at one time in her life at least she possessed three thousand dresses at once, or so historians tell us. In fact, Richmond Palace was called the Queen's wardrobe, being practically filled with her gowns that were not in use.

1 5 5 0—1 5 6 0 *(continued)*

With the introduction of new styles of head-dress the centre parting became less general. The hair was brushed back from the forehead rather loosely to make a slight puff round the face, and later was padded on either side so that it might fill the curve of the cap, as may be seen on the page facing. The heart-shaped cap, commonly associated with Mary Queen of Scots, became amazingly fashionable and continued in fashion with many slight alterations until caps ceased to be worn. They were at first worn over a small embroidered cap, as seen at the top of the previous page.

Heavily embroidered and jewelled bands of material seem to have been the most popular method of decoration for most garments, and of course *picadils* were still as popular. Bone-lace was also used a great deal, both as a trimming and as a hat-band for men. Heavy gold neck-chains were not as popular as the narrow cord or ribbon, with a locket attached ; the locket either carried a portrait of a lover, some precious stone, or a tiny miniature. Women wore similar cords tied round their waists, and on these a rosary was sometimes worn. Ear-rings were very popular for both sexes, the gallant often preferring to wear only one. Small ruffles were worn by practically everyone, for the huge turn-down collar became more popular in the 'sixties.

1560—1570

SOME account of the development of trunk-hose
has already been given, but this example conveys
a better idea of their actual structure than any written
explanation. In surviving contemporary specimens it is
not until those of the 'sixties that we can see with any
clearness how these trunk-hose were composed; but when
the jerkin no longer covers the doublet several excellent
examples are forthcoming. Although the *panes* are
clearly shown in the costume illustrated here, it should be
explained that the "drawings-out" were in most cases
definitely fuller than these. Sometimes as many as a dozen
yards of material were used in the stuffing of one pair,
and if this was particularly fine it was pulled out several
inches beyond the *panes*.

From about 1565 breeches began to assume gigantic
proportions, and, although the cut seems to have varied, the
common practice was to stuff them with bran, wool, hair,
rags, or anything else that might be at hand. Soldiers found
them particularly useful for storing loot. So absurdly large
did they become that a scaffold was erected in the Houses of
Parliament "for those to sit on who used the wearing of
great breeches stuffed with hair like wool sacks." Apparently it was impossible to sit with any degree of comfort on
an ordinary chair. What method was adopted in the home to
make seating possible it is difficult to say; there are no
records of chairs differing in structure, in fact existing
examples of Elizabethan furniture show us that few chairs
were without arms.

1560—1570 (*continued*)

In the year 1564 starch was introduced into England by a certain Mistress Dingham Vander Plasse. So great was the demand for education in starching that she started a school of instruction in the composition of starch, and charged several pounds for imparting this knowledge to young ladies of rank. The problem of laundering was solved, and ruffles began to grow enormously in size. But this knowledge took several years to filter down through the masses, and not until the 'seventies was the large " ruff " worn by everyone. There are several existing prints representing the laundering and forming of ruffs during the 'seventies and 'eighties of the sixteenth century.

Starch in its earliest days was tinted yellow, so that the first big ruffles were invariably creamy in colour. The fashion died, however, when a certain notorious Mrs. Turner was hanged at Tyburn in one of these yellow ruffles. After this gruesome episode the modish shade turned from yellow to blue, probably very little different in its palest tints from the starch we use to-day. Frequently the ruff was untied in front to give a little more air and freedom to the wearer, for it is difficult to imagine any form of neck-wear more uncomfortable than a closed ruff. Large upstanding collars were worn by women who did not favour the ruffle, and the turned-down collar already mentioned was worn by men. The neck was not visible again until the 'nineties of the century, but there are numerous instances of a gown itself finishing with a low, square line at the shoulders so that a considerable expanse of bare chest was visible under the ruffle and above the gown.

1560—1570 *(continued)*

During the year 1565 the problem of unemployment in cloth-manufacturing towns became chronic, because so many imported silks and velvets were used that there was little or no demand for the woollens and cottons manufactured in England. An appeal was made to the Queen, who issued a proclamation forbidding any further importation of materials from the Continent, and further ordering that every man should wear a woollen cap unless he had an income of over forty pounds a year. Whether these official commands made any impression on the people is difficult to say, but it is certain that the effect, if any, was not lasting, because garments, instead of losing brilliance, seem to have become even more rich and ornate than before. And the woollen cap was not nearly as popular as the velvet one, or as the more fashionable hat. If the Queen had followed up her proclamation by herself appearing in some woollen or cotton gown instead of the exaggerated foreign styles she invariably adopted, the royal decrees might have been more effective.

The first figure on the opposite page is wearing an excellent example of the Spanish *vertingale* or farthingale, and the general use of small slashes and picadils is shown. It is difficult to exaggerate the importance attached to details at this period : the garments illustrated here may appear comparatively simple, but in reality they were crowded with minute designs, lace, embroidery, guards and gold *aglets* (small eyelet holes for the " points ").

1560—1570 (continued)

A little may be said here about the wearing of beards in the Sixteenth Century. For the first twenty years of the period men were clean-shaven. Henry VIII, however, started to grow a beard at about the age of twenty-three, and a few years afterwards the mode became popular among the nobility. By 1545 the fashion had spread, and beards were far more prevalent than clean-shaven faces. The pointed beard and small pointed moustache first came into vogue during the 'fifties, probably another introduction from Spain by Philip. The beard became gradually smaller and neater until the 'nineties, and by about 1600 had assumed the size and shape of a small triangular postage-stamp stuck in the middle of the chin. Tiny moustaches with no beard were also fashionable from about 1570 to the end of the century.

The two upper head-dresses on opposite page are interesting in that they represent some of the amusing transitional stages between head-dresses and hats, the one on the right being distinctly reminiscent of the policeman's helmet of to-day. Men's hats with a large brim and a shallow crown were not worn for more than a few years in this decade ; they were followed by a craze for high crowns, but became popular again during the late 'eighties. Caps at this time had little or no brim, but a band of lace, embroidery, or jewels was usually worn as a form of decoration.

1570—1580

WITH the 'seventies came several entirely new fashions for men. The doublet began to develop a sort of padded and stiffened point in front, whence it was commonly known as the " peascod-belly " doublet, of which one of the earliest examples is illustrated here ; this fashion became ridiculously exaggerated during the 'eighties. The *mandilion* was almost as popular as the cloak ; it was a short, full coat or jerkin with hanging sleeves, the sides often split to show the doublet underneath. Cloaks were most fashionable, short, barely reaching to the hips, and sometimes worn swathed round in the Venetian style, as may be seen on the left-hand figure at the foot of the next page. Shoulder-padding was general, and " wings " were added to accentuate the width of the doublet.

Short stockings called boot-hose were worn under the boot to save the hose from unnecessary friction ; similar in shape to the golf-stocking of to-day, they were made of rich materials and beautifully embroidered. Venetians, a species of knee-breeches, bombasted, quilted, and padded, came into vogue about 1572. These usually reached just to the knee, and were either tied with a wide garter or finished with a small frill or band. Whenever trunk-hose were worn they were so abbreviated as barely to cover the buttocks, and as the peascod doublet became more exaggerated the trunks developed into a mere small roll a few inches deep, sometimes hardly visible under the huge doublet in front. It should be remembered here that after about 1550 the term " upper-stocks " was dropped in favour of the more general " trunk-hose," so that in describing hose the roll or pumpkin-like top was usually called " trunk-hose," and the leg covering itself termed " nether-stocks."

1 5 7 0—1 5 8 0 *(continued)*

About six or seven years after the introduction of " Venetians," yet another new style came into being—trunk-hose
with canions. A loose stocking-like appendage was attached
to the padded trunks and reached just below the knee ; the
nether-stocks were separate and drew up like a stocking over
the canions, fastening with a garter either just above or
below the knee. One of the earliest examples of this style
is to be seen on the lower left-hand figure on the
opposite page. An interesting variation of the trunk-hose,
especially amusing for its plus-fours appearance, is worn
by the upper left-hand figure. This variation was, however, of German or Swiss origin, and not frequently seen
in England. When this style was worn the padding was
all of loose material, not bombast, and the drawings-out
through the panes were sometimes so liberal that the panes
themselves were practically invisible.

Silks, velvets, satins, damasks, sarcenet, taffeta, and châlet
were the most popular materials. Although all these were
imported, the old trouble of unemployment in manufacturing
towns seems by this time to have been to some degree
avoided by the large export trade in wools, kerseys, dozens,
penistone cottons, fustians, buffins, cameleons, linsey-woolsey,
and many other interesting materials. All these apparently
were not suitable foundations for the exquisite tailoring and
abundant embroidery lavished on practically all English
garments at this time.

About this time Elizabeth was presented with a pair of
silk stockings woven by one of her ladies, and after wearing
these she decided to dispense with any other form of hose.
Whether she was actually the first person in England to wear
hand-knitted stockings it is difficult to say—there are records
of Edward VII having a pair of silk hose given him, and
apparently they were hand-knitted. However, after the
'sixties silk nether-stocks became exceedingly fashionable in
spite of the fact that as much as five pounds was paid for a
single pair.

1570—1580 (*continued*)

Women's clothes also became more exaggerated in style. One particularly new garment was the transparent cobweb lawn cloak or veil, with a large, upstanding, heart-shaped collar, in some cases closely resembling a hood. These cloaks or veils often reached to the ground, and were decorated with a tiny edge of lace.

Towards the end of this decade came the French *vertingale* or farthingale. This was vastly different from the Spanish vertingale in that the contour, instead of being cone-shaped, was more like that of a drum with the upper rim tilted down in the front. This effect was obtained with the help of a large whalebone frame of cart-wheel shape fitted to the hips and tipped up at the back by shortening the spoke-like attachments. The skirt worn over this was exceedingly full, and shorter than any other form of dress at this period. Sometimes a similar effect was obtained by the wearing of a bolster-like padding tied round the waist. There were many variations of this fashion : sometimes a short, loosely gathered basque was worn over the skirt finishing at the hoop, and later an immense ruffle, similar to the ones worn about the neck, was attached to the waist and reached out to the edge of the drum. The Spanish farthingale did not lose its popularity with the introduction of the French, and in some contemporary paintings we can see clearly that the skirt was sometimes held out by means of a single hoop at the hem and a little padding at the waist.

1570—1580 (continued)

Hats now began to assume a jaunty and, to us, an amusing aspect. Beaver—alluded to as a curious kind of hair—was quite popular by about 1578. Sarcenet, wool, taffeta, and velvet were all used in the making of hats. Ladies often wore them over a tight-fitting cap. The hat-band was a specially valuable possession, as this was frequently adorned with precious stones and pearls.

Contemporary moralists wrote scathingly of the absurdities of fashion, and particularly of the wickedness of using cosmetics. One such writer took it upon himself to deliver this awful warning: "Those which paint or colour themselves in this world otherwise than God hath made them, let them feare lest when the daie of judgement commeth the Lorde will not knowe them for his creatures."

Writers of this period seem to have been divided into two definite classes: Those who indulged in every possible extravagance and excuse for indecency in their literary efforts, and stern moralists who, in their somewhat wild efforts to crush extravagance, rigorously damned everything pertaining to beauty, cleanliness, fastidiousness, or general improvements. The former upheld the gaiety and brilliance of Court life, the feasting, drinking, and general debauchery, and they give us a fairly accurate account of the life of any young gallant who was not afraid to sow sufficient wild-oats to drive him out of his town, or even out of the country, for a few years.

1580—1590

THE peascod doublet reached the height, or depth, of absurdity during these ten years; after about 1590 few exaggerated styles were to be seen. Not only were these doublets exceedingly hot and bulky for the unfortunate wearer, but he experienced great difficulty in any endeavour to stoop. So stuffed, bombasted, and quilted did they become that the points actually reached some eight or nine inches below the belt. The idea of the unitiated appears to have been that these doublets were designed especially to further " gourmandie and gluttonie." As eating and drinking was one of the chief pastimes during the latter part of the century, there may have been some truth in so sweeping an assertion, and consideration of the figures illustrated on the next page makes it easy to sympathize with this view. When we read of the amazing dishes of capons, larks, sparrows, roast oxen, boars' heads, and innumerable pies—including, of course, the then rare delicacy, " potato pyes "—that were habitually consumed at one sitting, it is hard to avoid believing that some sort of camouflage for undue stoutness was necessary.

The Anatomie of Abuses suggests that the exaggerated fashions worn at this time were not altogether approved, even by their wearers : " For moste of our new-fangled fashions dooe thei not rather deforme us than adorne us, disguise us than become us, makyng us rather semble savage Beastes and sterne monsters than continent sober christians ? " Probably this reasonable point of view accounts for the comparatively short popularity of the peascod belly in this country. Nevertheless it is the period immortalized by Punch and Judy, for even to-day Punch may be seen with his ruffle and peascod doublet.

1580—1590 (*continued*)

Women started to frizz and crimp their hair during the 'eighties, and, as the " puffed " effect grew in favour, wire frames were devised to support their frizzed and curled locks. " Wreaths " and " borders " were arranged across the top of the head from ear to ear ; these were sometimes imitation flowers, or even precious stones set in a gold or silver framework. Wigs and added pieces of hair became popular, and dyes were used so extensively that a lady of fashion was rarely seen at two succeeding functions with her hair the same shade. As additional decorations, rings, beads, pearls, precious stones, and other gewgaws were fixed among the curls in a manner called enchanting by contemporaries. The hair apparently became a nesting-place for any extra piece of jewellery that could not be affixed elsewhere.

Elizabeth herself specialized in wigs, red and a sort of saffron colour being her two favourite shades. Some fashionable ladies not blessed with such an abundance of hair as their more fortunate sisters, and probably unwilling to go to the expense of buying wigs, bribed peasant women and children to part with their locks for a few pence, and thus added to their inadequate supply of crowning glory. The hair being eventually arranged or " laid out " to the wearer's satisfaction, a large velvet or beaver hat was perched on the front or side of the head ; these hats were similar to those worn by men and invariably had a feather worn in the hat-band.

1580—1590 (continued)

It will be noticed that whenever the French farthingale was worn a stiff V-shaped stomacher invariably accompanied it. This was worn at a slight angle to the body, fitting at the breast and gradually sloping outwards, till the base of the V rested on the tilted front of the farthingale. In several portraits of the time the hand is hidden behind this, which means that in some cases the stomacher must have been worn loose. Tight-lacing was exceedingly prevalent, and there are records that " since busks came in request horn is scarce." Girls endeavoured to make their waists so small that they could span them with their hands. This wasp-waist outline was augmented by the use, above and below the corset, of " little bolsters or pillows for to seem more fat and comely." The shoulders were padded and the sleeves bombasted in violent contrast to the small waist.

Ruffles during the 'eighties became so large and unwieldy that an under-prop was devised to lift them up. Sometimes the ruffle was pinned to the ears ; in other instances it fell down over the shoulders.

Cork-soled shoes called *pinsnets* and *pantoffles* were worn ; these had a heel about an inch or an inch and a half high, and their wearers had great difficulty in managing to walk with them. So uncomfortable were they that frequently men's legs swelled from wearing them. Every possible colour and material was used in the making of these shoes.

Hose made from jernsey, worsted, crewell, yarn, thread, and of course the most fashionable silk, were dyed as many different colours as the shoes. An interesting list of fashionable shades includes " russet, saffron, black, white, red, grene, yellowe, watchet, blew and pink." Scabbards and sheaths were made from velvet and even embroidered linen.

1580—1590 (*continued*)

Ladies at this time wore beautifully embroidered and scented gloves and shoes or " pumps " made of cheverill, silk, or velvet. When walking abroad they carried black velvet masks to shield their complexions from the sun, or to disguise them from undesirable acquaintances. Fans with silver handles were very popular, and practically every woman carried a small hand-mirror either attached to her girdle or hanging on a cord about her neck. These looking-glasses were rudely alluded to as " Devil's Spectacles " by contemporary moralists—" And good reason, else how could they see the devil in themselves ? "

Apparently rather childish and demure mannerisms, and a craze for " baby-talk," were adopted by the most fashionable ladies. These must have seemed more than a little absurd, and in violent contrast to their stiff, bombasted appearances— and, by all accounts, their ultra-sophisticated and immoral behaviour. Let it be said at once that at least Elizabeth did not set the vogue for " baby-talk " ; her vocabulary would probably shock even the broadest-minded of men of to-day. Shakespeare does not give the impression that a mincing of words was the general trend of the time, and his works are amazingly discreet compared with others written at the same period. Men were certainly somewhat coarse in their behaviour, even if effeminate in their apparel : spitting, tobacco - chewing, and tooth - picking were all reckoned elegant accomplishments.

1590—1600

THE century ends in a wild orgy of extravagance. Even the country people, previously content with their russet smocks and *mockados*, now emulated their superiors in every conceivable manner and blossomed out in silks and satins whenever in any way possible, selling their last cow or pig to buy a pair of fine silk hose to excite the envy of their less well-apparelled neighbours. Clothes seem to have become the principal consideration in life, and so many and varied were the styles for men that the fop or gallant could hardly have one suit completed before it was out of fashion. In Ben Jonson's *Everyman out of his Humour*, the young collegiate tries desperately to keep pace with the latest demands of fashion, and in consequence gets head-over-heels in debt, because as fast as his tailor turns out one style he sees another which is newer and therefore more desirable. The fashionable lady is seen vividly and entertainingly through the eyes of a contemporary poet :

> . . . Wear curled Periwigs and chalk their faces
> And still are gazing in their pocket glasses.
> Tyred with pinned ruffles, fans and partlet-strips
> With Buskes and Vertingales about their hips.
> And tread on Corked Stilts at pris'nor's pace,
> And make their napkin for their spitting place.

The whole century was such a comical mixture of polished indecency and crude exquisiteness that it is only after reading dozens of contemporary volumes that we can hope to obtain even a glimmering understanding of these ancestors of ours. Doubtless an Elizabethan gentleman landed suddenly amongst us to-day would consider our modes and manners equally inconsistent and amusing.

The magnificent costume illustrated here provides an interesting example of sixteenth-century design. Some time during the 'eighties a fashion for depicting scenes, animals, birds, fishes, or anything which might be a typical emblem of the wearer, had been adopted as a motif for design. This particular petticoat—drawn from a garment belonging to Elizabeth—is probably intended to show some of the beasts, flowers, fish, and fowl to be found in her dominions, and the foreign waters explored by her sea captains. There is also an existing portrait of Sir Francis Drake, in the National Portrait Gallery, apparently painted soon after his circumnavigation, which clearly shows small worlds, each encircled by a complete ring, embroidered on his doublet.

1590—1600 (*continued*)

Ladies' stomachers or doublets were often cut from the same pattern as men's, and even at this early date we find the now time-worn assertion that women were aping men, and trying to appear masculine to the detriment of their natural charms. Though how a richly embroidered doublet with a lace-edged ruffle, worn over exaggeratedly full skirts, could be termed masculine it is difficult to comprehend.

Men's hair was worn frequently shoulder-length, and about 1595 a fashion for " ear-locks "—later termed love-locks—became very popular with young men. The hair in this case was allowed to grow in front so that it hung down in two locks, one either side of the face, and rested in a curl on each shoulder ; the back, however, was kept short.

Practically any shape or size of hat might be fashionable during the 'nineties. High-crowned and small-brimmed, or low-crowned and large-brimmed, were each equally smart if worn with a cable hat-band. Some crowns were so high that they rose twelve or fifteen inches above the head. All colours and practically any material might be used in the making up of these hats.

1590—1600 (*continued*)

Trunk-hose with canions assumed two definite formations. One, the unbroken roll round the hips, as seen on several earlier pages, and the other somewhat square in effect, slightly resembling a miniature farthingale ; three of these will be seen on the previous page. *Panes* either developed into a formal series of embroidered bands, with nothing of the padding or lining visible, or else became sufficiently small and narrow for the drawings-out to be evenly arranged to cover them. The latter arrangement gave the appearance of an equally-gathered piece of material, as is shown in the last coloured plate.

The skirt of the doublet at this time was cut up to form overlapping tabs similar in appearance to the " tassets " worn on armour. One other form of breeches that became a " rage " during the last decade of the century were the " open-breeches." These were perfectly straight, un-gathered trousers, that reached a few inches below the knees, similar in cut to a rather elongated pair of modern shorts, or an abbreviated pair of trousers. Usually these were embroidered, and a tendency to decorate the hem with coloured ribbon or bone-lace ultimately developed into the lace-edged, flapping nether-garments of the Cavalier of the Stuart period.

1590—1600 (*continued*)

So we draw to the close of the most interesting century in our history, a century shaken by the discovery of a New World, yielding untold wealth for any man to exploit. The people, in their crazed enthusiasm over the New World, burst into wild orgies of expenditure. Illimitable adventure awaited them across the seas. Why should they be afraid of adventure in their own country ? If a fortune were gambled away in one single night, what matter ? Could not they sail forth, as others had done, to an unknown El Dorado, and come back in galleons laden with all manner of precious stones and great bars of gold and silver ? No sober-minded stay-at-homes were they. And the spirit of adventure, bravery, and extravagance must needs be given expression— hence the dazzling array of costumes, the exotic materials, and the priceless decorations set forth in these pages.

A CATALOG OF SELECTED
DOVER BOOKS
IN ALL FIELDS OF INTEREST

A CATALOG OF SELECTED DOVER
BOOKS IN ALL FIELDS OF INTEREST

CONCERNING THE SPIRITUAL IN ART, Wassily Kandinsky. Pioneering work by father of abstract art. Thoughts on color theory, nature of art. Analysis of earlier masters. 12 illustrations. 80pp. of text. 5⅜ x 8½.   23411-8 Pa. $4.95

ANIMALS: 1,419 Copyright-Free Illustrations of Mammals, Birds, Fish, Insects, etc., Jim Harter (ed.). Clear wood engravings present, in extremely lifelike poses, over 1,000 species of animals. One of the most extensive pictorial sourcebooks of its kind. Captions. Index. 284pp. 9 x 12.   23766-4 Pa. $14.95

CELTIC ART: The Methods of Construction, George Bain. Simple geometric techniques for making Celtic interlacements, spirals, Kells-type initials, animals, humans, etc. Over 500 illustrations. 160pp. 9 x 12. (USO)   22923-8 Pa. $9.95

AN ATLAS OF ANATOMY FOR ARTISTS, Fritz Schider. Most thorough reference work on art anatomy in the world. Hundreds of illustrations, including selections from works by Vesalius, Leonardo, Goya, Ingres, Michelangelo, others. 593 illustrations. 192pp. 7⅛ x 10¼.   20241-0 Pa. $9.95

CELTIC HAND STROKE-BY-STROKE (Irish Half-Uncial from "The Book of Kells"): An Arthur Baker Calligraphy Manual, Arthur Baker. Complete guide to creating each letter of the alphabet in distinctive Celtic manner. Covers hand position, strokes, pens, inks, paper, more. Illustrated. 48pp. 8¼ x 11.   24336-2 Pa. $3.95

EASY ORIGAMI, John Montroll. Charming collection of 32 projects (hat, cup, pelican, piano, swan, many more) specially designed for the novice origami hobbyist. Clearly illustrated easy-to-follow instructions insure that even beginning paper-crafters will achieve successful results. 48pp. 8¼ x 11.   27298-2 Pa. $3.50

THE COMPLETE BOOK OF BIRDHOUSE CONSTRUCTION FOR WOOD-WORKERS, Scott D. Campbell. Detailed instructions, illustrations, tables. Also data on bird habitat and instinct patterns. Bibliography. 3 tables. 63 illustrations in 15 figures. 48pp. 5¼ x 8½.   24407-5 Pa. $2.50

BLOOMINGDALE'S ILLUSTRATED 1886 CATALOG: Fashions, Dry Goods and Housewares, Bloomingdale Brothers. Famed merchants' extremely rare catalog depicting about 1,700 products: clothing, housewares, firearms, dry goods, jewelry, more. Invaluable for dating, identifying vintage items. Also, copyright-free graphics for artists, designers. Co-published with Henry Ford Museum & Greenfield Village. 160pp. 8¼ x 11.   25780-0 Pa. $10.95

HISTORIC COSTUME IN PICTURES, Braun & Schneider. Over 1,450 costumed figures in clearly detailed engravings—from dawn of civilization to end of 19th century. Captions. Many folk costumes. 256pp. 8⅜ x 11¾.   23150-X Pa. $12.95

MY BONDAGE AND MY FREEDOM, Frederick Douglass. Born a slave, Douglass became outspoken force in antislavery movement. The best of Douglass' autobiographies. Graphic description of slave life. 464pp. 5⅜ x 8½. 22457-0 Pa. $8.95

FOLLOWING THE EQUATOR: A Journey Around the World, Mark Twain. Fascinating humorous account of 1897 voyage to Hawaii, Australia, India, New Zealand, etc. Ironic, bemused reports on peoples, customs, climate, flora and fauna, politics, much more. 197 illustrations. 720pp. 5⅜ x 8½. 26113-1 Pa. $15.95

THE PEOPLE CALLED SHAKERS, Edward D. Andrews. Definitive study of Shakers: origins, beliefs, practices, dances, social organization, furniture and crafts, etc. 33 illustrations. 351pp. 5⅜ x 8½. 21081-2 Pa. $8.95

THE MYTHS OF GREECE AND ROME, H. A. Guerber. A classic of mythology, generously illustrated, long prized for its simple, graphic, accurate retelling of the principal myths of Greece and Rome, and for its commentary on their origins and significance. With 64 illustrations by Michelangelo, Raphael, Titian, Rubens, Canova, Bernini and others. 480pp. 5⅜ x 8½. 27584-1 Pa. $9.95

PSYCHOLOGY OF MUSIC, Carl E. Seashore. Classic work discusses music as a medium from psychological viewpoint. Clear treatment of physical acoustics, auditory apparatus, sound perception, development of musical skills, nature of musical feeling, host of other topics. 88 figures. 408pp. 5⅜ x 8½. 21851-1 Pa. $11.95

THE PHILOSOPHY OF HISTORY, Georg W. Hegel. Great classic of Western thought develops concept that history is not chance but rational process, the evolution of freedom. 457pp. 5⅜ x 8½. 20112-0 Pa. $9.95

THE BOOK OF TEA, Kakuzo Okakura. Minor classic of the Orient: entertaining, charming explanation, interpretation of traditional Japanese culture in terms of tea ceremony. 94pp. 5⅜ x 8½. 20070-1 Pa. $3.95

LIFE IN ANCIENT EGYPT, Adolf Erman. Fullest, most thorough, detailed older account with much not in more recent books, domestic life, religion, magic, medicine, commerce, much more. Many illustrations reproduce tomb paintings, carvings, hieroglyphs, etc. 597pp. 5⅜ x 8½. 22632-8 Pa. $12.95

SUNDIALS, Their Theory and Construction, Albert Waugh. Far and away the best, most thorough coverage of ideas, mathematics concerned, types, construction, adjusting anywhere. Simple, nontechnical treatment allows even children to build several of these dials. Over 100 illustrations. 230pp. 5⅜ x 8½. 22947-5 Pa. $8.95

DYNAMICS OF FLUIDS IN POROUS MEDIA, Jacob Bear. For advanced students of ground water hydrology, soil mechanics and physics, drainage and irrigation engineering, and more. 335 illustrations. Exercises, with answers. 784pp. 6⅛ x 9¼. 65675-6 Pa. $19.95

SONGS OF EXPERIENCE: Facsimile Reproduction with 26 Plates in Full Color, William Blake. 26 full-color plates from a rare 1826 edition. Includes "TheTyger," "London," "Holy Thursday," and other poems. Printed text of poems. 48pp. 5¼ x 7. 24636-1 Pa. $4.95

OLD-TIME VIGNETTES IN FULL COLOR, Carol Belanger Grafton (ed.). Over 390 charming, often sentimental illustrations, selected from archives of Victorian graphics—pretty women posing, children playing, food, flowers, kittens and puppies, smiling cherubs, birds and butterflies, much more. All copyright-free. 48pp. 9¼ x 12¼. 27269-9 Pa. $7.95

PERSPECTIVE FOR ARTISTS, Rex Vicat Cole. Depth, perspective of sky and sea, shadows, much more, not usually covered. 391 diagrams, 81 reproductions of drawings and paintings. 279pp. 5⅜ x 8½. 22487-2 Pa. $7.95

DRAWING THE LIVING FIGURE, Joseph Sheppard. Innovative approach to artistic anatomy focuses on specifics of surface anatomy, rather than muscles and bones. Over 170 drawings of live models in front, back and side views, and in widely varying poses. Accompanying diagrams. 177 illustrations. Introduction. Index. 144pp. 8⅜ x11¼. 26723-7 Pa. $8.95

GOTHIC AND OLD ENGLISH ALPHABETS: 100 Complete Fonts, Dan X. Solo. Add power, elegance to posters, signs, other graphics with 100 stunning copyright-free alphabets: Blackstone, Dolbey, Germania, 97 more–including many lower-case, numerals, punctuation marks. 104pp. 8⅛ x 11. 24695-7 Pa. $8.95

HOW TO DO BEADWORK, Mary White. Fundamental book on craft from simple projects to five-bead chains and woven works. 106 illustrations. 142pp. 5⅜ x 8. 20697-1 Pa. $5.95

THE BOOK OF WOOD CARVING, Charles Marshall Sayers. Finest book for beginners discusses fundamentals and offers 34 designs. "Absolutely first rate . . . well thought out and well executed."–E. J. Tangerman. 118pp. 7¾ x 10⅝. 23654-4 Pa. $7.95

ILLUSTRATED CATALOG OF CIVIL WAR MILITARY GOODS: Union Army Weapons, Insignia, Uniform Accessories, and Other Equipment, Schuyler, Hartley, and Graham. Rare, profusely illustrated 1846 catalog includes Union Army uniform and dress regulations, arms and ammunition, coats, insignia, flags, swords, rifles, etc. 226 illustrations. 160pp. 9 x 12. 24939-5 Pa. $10.95

WOMEN'S FASHIONS OF THE EARLY 1900s: An Unabridged Republication of "New York Fashions, 1909," National Cloak & Suit Co. Rare catalog of mail-order fashions documents women's and children's clothing styles shortly after the turn of the century. Captions offer full descriptions, prices. Invaluable resource for fashion, costume historians. Approximately 725 illustrations. 128pp. 8⅜ x 11¼. 27276-1 Pa. $11.95

THE 1912 AND 1915 GUSTAV STICKLEY FURNITURE CATALOGS, Gustav Stickley. With over 200 detailed illustrations and descriptions, these two catalogs are essential reading and reference materials and identification guides for Stickley furniture. Captions cite materials, dimensions and prices. 112pp. 6½ x 9¼. 26676-1 Pa. $9.95

EARLY AMERICAN LOCOMOTIVES, John H. White, Jr. Finest locomotive engravings from early 19th century: historical (1804–74), main-line (after 1870), special, foreign, etc. 147 plates. 142pp. 11⅜ x 8¼. 22772-3 Pa. $10.95

THE TALL SHIPS OF TODAY IN PHOTOGRAPHS, Frank O. Braynard. Lavishly illustrated tribute to nearly 100 majestic contemporary sailing vessels: Amerigo Vespucci, Clearwater, Constitution, Eagle, Mayflower, Sea Cloud, Victory, many more. Authoritative captions provide statistics, background on each ship. 190 black-and-white photographs and illustrations. Introduction. 128pp. 8⅞ x 11¾. 27163-3 Pa. $14.95

EARLY NINETEENTH-CENTURY CRAFTS AND TRADES, Peter Stockham (ed.). Extremely rare 1807 volume describes to youngsters the crafts and trades of the day: brickmaker, weaver, dressmaker, bookbinder, ropemaker, saddler, many more. Quaint prose, charming illustrations for each craft. 20 black-and-white line illustrations. 192pp. 4⅝ x 6. 27293-1 Pa. $4.95

VICTORIAN FASHIONS AND COSTUMES FROM HARPER'S BAZAR, 1867–1898, Stella Blum (ed.). Day costumes, evening wear, sports clothes, shoes, hats, other accessories in over 1,000 detailed engravings. 320pp. 9⅜ x 12¼.
22990-4 Pa. $15.95

GUSTAV STICKLEY, THE CRAFTSMAN, Mary Ann Smith. Superb study surveys broad scope of Stickley's achievement, especially in architecture. Design philosophy, rise and fall of the Craftsman empire, descriptions and floor plans for many Craftsman houses, more. 86 black-and-white halftones. 31 line illustrations. Introduction 208pp. 6½ x 9¼. 27210-9 Pa. $9.95

THE LONG ISLAND RAIL ROAD IN EARLY PHOTOGRAPHS, Ron Ziel. Over 220 rare photos, informative text document origin (1844) and development of rail service on Long Island. Vintage views of early trains, locomotives, stations, passengers, crews, much more. Captions. 8⅞ x 11¾. 26301-0 Pa. $13.95

THE BOOK OF OLD SHIPS: From Egyptian Galleys to Clipper Ships, Henry B. Culver. Superb, authoritative history of sailing vessels, with 80 magnificent line illustrations. Galley, bark, caravel, longship, whaler, many more. Detailed, informative text on each vessel by noted naval historian. Introduction. 256pp. 5⅜ x 8½.
27332-6 Pa. $7.95

TEN BOOKS ON ARCHITECTURE, Vitruvius. The most important book ever written on architecture. Early Roman aesthetics, technology, classical orders, site selection, all other aspects. Morgan translation. 331pp. 5⅜ x 8½. 20645-9 Pa. $8.95

THE HUMAN FIGURE IN MOTION, Eadweard Muybridge. More than 4,500 stopped-action photos, in action series, showing undraped men, women, children jumping, lying down, throwing, sitting, wrestling, carrying, etc. 390pp. 7⅞ x 10⅝.
20204-6 Clothbd. $27.95

TREES OF THE EASTERN AND CENTRAL UNITED STATES AND CANADA, William M. Harlow. Best one-volume guide to 140 trees. Full descriptions, woodlore, range, etc. Over 600 illustrations. Handy size. 288pp. 4½ x 6⅜.
20395-6 Pa. $6.95

SONGS OF WESTERN BIRDS, Dr. Donald J. Borror. Complete song and call repertoire of 60 western species, including flycatchers, juncoes, cactus wrens, many more–includes fully illustrated booklet. Cassette and manual 99913-0 $8.95

GROWING AND USING HERBS AND SPICES, Milo Miloradovich. Versatile handbook provides all the information needed for cultivation and use of all the herbs and spices available in North America. 4 illustrations. Index. Glossary. 236pp. 5⅜ x 8½.
25058-X Pa. $7.95

BIG BOOK OF MAZES AND LABYRINTHS, Walter Shepherd. 50 mazes and labyrinths in all–classical, solid, ripple, and more–in one great volume. Perfect inexpensive puzzler for clever youngsters. Full solutions. 112pp. 8⅛ x 11.
22951-3 Pa. $4.95

PIANO TUNING, J. Cree Fischer. Clearest, best book for beginner, amateur. Simple repairs, raising dropped notes, tuning by easy method of flattened fifths. No previous skills needed. 4 illustrations. 201pp. 5⅜ x 8½. 23267-0 Pa. $6.95

A SOURCE BOOK IN THEATRICAL HISTORY, A. M. Nagler. Contemporary observers on acting, directing, make-up, costuming, stage props, machinery, scene design, from Ancient Greece to Chekhov. 611pp. 5⅜ x 8½. 20515-0 Pa. $12.95

THE COMPLETE NONSENSE OF EDWARD LEAR, Edward Lear. All nonsense limericks, zany alphabets, Owl and Pussycat, songs, nonsense botany, etc., illustrated by Lear. Total of 320pp. 5⅜ x 8½. (USO) 20167-8 Pa. $7.95

VICTORIAN PARLOUR POETRY: An Annotated Anthology, Michael R. Turner. 117 gems by Longfellow, Tennyson, Browning, many lesser-known poets. "The Village Blacksmith," "Curfew Must Not Ring Tonight," "Only a Baby Small," dozens more, often difficult to find elsewhere. Index of poets, titles, first lines. xxiii + 325pp. 5⅜ x 8¼. 27044-0 Pa. $8.95

DUBLINERS, James Joyce. Fifteen stories offer vivid, tightly focused observations of the lives of Dublin's poorer classes. At least one, "The Dead," is considered a masterpiece. Reprinted complete and unabridged from standard edition. 160pp. 5³⁄₁₆ x 8¼. 26870-5 Pa. $1.00

THE HAUNTED MONASTERY and THE CHINESE MAZE MURDERS, Robert van Gulik. Two full novels by van Gulik, set in 7th-century China, continue adventures of Judge Dee and his companions. An evil Taoist monastery, seemingly supernatural events; overgrown topiary maze hides strange crimes. 27 illustrations. 328pp. 5⅜ x 8½. 23502-5 Pa. $8.95

THE BOOK OF THE SACRED MAGIC OF ABRAMELIN THE MAGE, translated by S. MacGregor Mathers. Medieval manuscript of ceremonial magic. Basic document in Aleister Crowley, Golden Dawn groups. 268pp. 5⅜ x 8½. 23211-5 Pa. $9.95

NEW RUSSIAN-ENGLISH AND ENGLISH-RUSSIAN DICTIONARY, M. A. O'Brien. This is a remarkably handy Russian dictionary, containing a surprising amount of information, including over 70,000 entries. 366pp. 4½ x 6⅛. 20208-9 Pa. $10.95

HISTORIC HOMES OF THE AMERICAN PRESIDENTS, Second, Revised Edition, Irvin Haas. A traveler's guide to American Presidential homes, most open to the public, depicting and describing homes occupied by every American President from George Washington to George Bush. With visiting hours, admission charges, travel routes. 175 photographs. Index. 160pp. 8¼ x 11. 26751-2 Pa. $11.95

NEW YORK IN THE FORTIES, Andreas Feininger. 162 brilliant photographs by the well-known photographer, formerly with *Life* magazine. Commuters, shoppers, Times Square at night, much else from city at its peak. Captions by John von Hartz. 181pp. 9¼ x 10¾. 23585-8 Pa. $13.95

INDIAN SIGN LANGUAGE, William Tomkins. Over 525 signs developed by Sioux and other tribes. Written instructions and diagrams. Also 290 pictographs. 111pp. 6⅛ x 9¼. 22029-X Pa. $3.95

ANATOMY: A Complete Guide for Artists, Joseph Sheppard. A master of figure drawing shows artists how to render human anatomy convincingly. Over 460 illustrations. 224pp. 8⅜ x 11¼. 27279-6 Pa. $11.95

MEDIEVAL CALLIGRAPHY: Its History and Technique, Marc Drogin. Spirited history, comprehensive instruction manual covers 13 styles (ca. 4th century thru 15th). Excellent photographs; directions for duplicating medieval techniques with modern tools. 224pp. 8⅜ x 11¼. 26142-5 Pa. $12.95

DRIED FLOWERS: How to Prepare Them, Sarah Whitlock and Martha Rankin. Complete instructions on how to use silica gel, meal and borax, perlite aggregate, sand and borax, glycerine and water to create attractive permanent flower arrangements. 12 illustrations. 32pp. 5⅜ x 8½. 21802-3 Pa. $1.00

EASY-TO-MAKE BIRD FEEDERS FOR WOODWORKERS, Scott D. Campbell. Detailed, simple-to-use guide for designing, constructing, caring for and using feeders. Text, illustrations for 12 classic and contemporary designs. 96pp. 5⅜ x 8½. 25847-5 Pa. $3.95

SCOTTISH WONDER TALES FROM MYTH AND LEGEND, Donald A. Mackenzie. 16 lively tales tell of giants rumbling down mountainsides, of a magic wand that turns stone pillars into warriors, of gods and goddesses, evil hags, powerful forces and more. 240pp. 5⅜ x 8½. 29677-6 Pa. $6.95

THE HISTORY OF UNDERCLOTHES, C. Willett Cunnington and Phyllis Cunnington. Fascinating, well-documented survey covering six centuries of English undergarments, enhanced with over 100 illustrations: 12th-century laced-up bodice, footed long drawers (1795), 19th-century bustles, l9th-century corsets for men, Victorian "bust improvers," much more. 272pp. 5⅜ x 8¼. 27124-2 Pa. $9.95

ARTS AND CRAFTS FURNITURE: The Complete Brooks Catalog of 1912, Brooks Manufacturing Co. Photos and detailed descriptions of more than 150 now very collectible furniture designs from the Arts and Crafts movement depict davenports, settees, buffets, desks, tables, chairs, bedsteads, dressers and more, all built of solid, quarter-sawed oak. Invaluable for students and enthusiasts of antiques, Americana and the decorative arts. 80pp. 6½ x 9¼. 27471-3 Pa. $8.95

HOW WE INVENTED THE AIRPLANE: An Illustrated History, Orville Wright. Fascinating firsthand account covers early experiments, construction of planes and motors, first flights, much more. Introduction and commentary by Fred C. Kelly. 76 photographs. 96pp. 8¼ x 11. 25662-6 Pa. $8.95

THE ARTS OF THE SAILOR: Knotting, Splicing and Ropework, Hervey Garrett Smith. Indispensable shipboard reference covers tools, basic knots and useful hitches; handsewing and canvas work, more. Over 100 illustrations. Delightful reading for sea lovers. 256pp. 5⅜ x 8½. 26440-8 Pa. $8.95

FRANK LLOYD WRIGHT'S FALLINGWATER: The House and Its History, Second, Revised Edition, Donald Hoffmann. A total revision—both in text and illustrations—of the standard document on Fallingwater, the boldest, most personal architectural statement of Wright's mature years, updated with valuable new material from the recently opened Frank Lloyd Wright Archives. "Fascinating"–*The New York Times*. 116 illustrations. 128pp. 9¼ x 10¾. 27430-6 Pa. $12.95

CATALOG OF DOVER BOOKS

PHOTOGRAPHIC SKETCHBOOK OF THE CIVIL WAR, Alexander Gardner. 100 photos taken on field during the Civil War. Famous shots of Manassas Harper's Ferry, Lincoln, Richmond, slave pens, etc. 244pp. 10⅝ x 8¼.   22731-6 Pa. $10.95

FIVE ACRES AND INDEPENDENCE, Maurice G. Kains. Great back-to-the-land classic explains basics of self-sufficient farming. The one book to get. 95 illustrations. 397pp. 5⅜ x 8½.   20974-1 Pa. $7.95

SONGS OF EASTERN BIRDS, Dr. Donald J. Borror. Songs and calls of 60 species most common to eastern U.S.: warblers, woodpeckers, flycatchers, thrushes, larks, many more in high-quality recording.   Cassette and manual 99912-2 $9.95

A MODERN HERBAL, Margaret Grieve. Much the fullest, most exact, most useful compilation of herbal material. Gigantic alphabetical encyclopedia, from aconite to zedoary, gives botanical information, medical properties, folklore, economic uses, much else. Indispensable to serious reader. 161 illustrations. 888pp. 6½ x 9¼. 2-vol. set. (USO)   Vol. I: 22798-7 Pa. $9.95
Vol. II: 22799-5 Pa. $9.95

HIDDEN TREASURE MAZE BOOK, Dave Phillips. Solve 34 challenging mazes accompanied by heroic tales of adventure. Evil dragons, people-eating plants, blood-thirsty giants, many more dangerous adversaries lurk at every twist and turn. 34 mazes, stories, solutions. 48pp. 8¼ x 11.   24566-7 Pa. $2.95

LETTERS OF W. A. MOZART, Wolfgang A. Mozart. Remarkable letters show bawdy wit, humor, imagination, musical insights, contemporary musical world; includes some letters from Leopold Mozart. 276pp. 5⅜ x 8½.   22859-2 Pa. $7.95

BASIC PRINCIPLES OF CLASSICAL BALLET, Agrippina Vaganova. Great Russian theoretician, teacher explains methods for teaching classical ballet. 118 illustrations. 175pp. 5⅜ x 8½.   22036-2 Pa. $5.95

THE JUMPING FROG, Mark Twain. Revenge edition. The original story of The Celebrated Jumping Frog of Calaveras County, a hapless French translation, and Twain's hilarious "retranslation" from the French. 12 illustrations. 66pp. 5⅜ x 8½.   22686-7 Pa. $3.95

BEST REMEMBERED POEMS, Martin Gardner (ed.). The 126 poems in this superb collection of 19th- and 20th-century British and American verse range from Shelley's "To a Skylark" to the impassioned "Renascence" of Edna St. Vincent Millay and to Edward Lear's whimsical "The Owl and the Pussycat." 224pp. 5⅜ x 8½.   27165-X Pa. $5.95

COMPLETE SONNETS, William Shakespeare. Over 150 exquisite poems deal with love, friendship, the tyranny of time, beauty's evanescence, death and other themes in language of remarkable power, precision and beauty. Glossary of archaic terms. 80pp. 5³⁄₁₆ x 8¼.   26686-9 Pa. $1.00

BODIES IN A BOOKSHOP, R. T. Campbell. Challenging mystery of blackmail and murder with ingenious plot and superbly drawn characters. In the best tradition of British suspense fiction. 192pp. 5⅜ x 8½.   24720-1 Pa. $6.95

THE INFLUENCE OF SEA POWER UPON HISTORY, 1660–1783, A. T. Mahan. Influential classic of naval history and tactics still used as text in war colleges. First paperback edition. 4 maps. 24 battle plans. 640pp. 5⅜ x 8½.   25509-3 Pa. $14.95

THE STORY OF THE TITANIC AS TOLD BY ITS SURVIVORS, Jack Winocour (ed.). What it was really like. Panic, despair, shocking inefficiency, and a little heroism. More thrilling than any fictional account. 26 illustrations. 320pp. 5⅜ x 8½.
20610-6 Pa. $8.95

FAIRY AND FOLK TALES OF THE IRISH PEASANTRY, William Butler Yeats (ed.). Treasury of 64 tales from the twilight world of Celtic myth and legend: "The Soul Cages," "The Kildare Pooka," "King O'Toole and his Goose," many more. Introduction and Notes by W. B. Yeats. 352pp. 5⅜ x 8½.   26941-8 Pa. $8.95

BUDDHIST MAHAYANA TEXTS, E. B. Cowell and Others (eds.). Superb, accurate translations of basic documents in Mahayana Buddhism, highly important in history of religions. The Buddha-karita of Asvaghosha, Larger Sukhavativyuha, more. 448pp. 5⅜ x 8½.   25552-2 Pa. $12.95

ONE TWO THREE . . . INFINITY: Facts and Speculations of Science, George Gamow. Great physicist's fascinating, readable overview of contemporary science: number theory, relativity, fourth dimension, entropy, genes, atomic structure, much more. 128 illustrations. Index. 352pp. 5⅜ x 8½.   25664-2 Pa. $8.95

ENGINEERING IN HISTORY, Richard Shelton Kirby, et al. Broad, nontechnical survey of history's major technological advances: birth of Greek science, industrial revolution, electricity and applied science, 20th-century automation, much more. 181 illustrations. ". . . excellent . . ."–Isis. Bibliography. vii + 530pp. 5⅜ x 8¼.
26412-2 Pa. $14.95

DALÍ ON MODERN ART: The Cuckolds of Antiquated Modern Art, Salvador Dalí. Influential painter skewers modern art and its practitioners. Outrageous evaluations of Picasso, Cézanne, Turner, more. 15 renderings of paintings discussed. 44 calligraphic decorations by Dalí. 96pp. 5⅜ x 8½. (USO)   29220-7 Pa. $4.95

ANTIQUE PLAYING CARDS: A Pictorial History, Henry René D'Allemagne. Over 900 elaborate, decorative images from rare playing cards (14th–20th centuries): Bacchus, death, dancing dogs, hunting scenes, royal coats of arms, players cheating, much more. 96pp. 9¼ x 12¼.   29265-7 Pa. $12.95

MAKING FURNITURE MASTERPIECES: 30 Projects with Measured Drawings, Franklin H. Gottshall. Step-by-step instructions, illustrations for constructing handsome, useful pieces, among them a Sheraton desk, Chippendale chair, Spanish desk, Queen Anne table and a William and Mary dressing mirror. 224pp. 8⅛ x 11¼.
29338-6 Pa. $13.95

THE FOSSIL BOOK: A Record of Prehistoric Life, Patricia V. Rich et al. Profusely illustrated definitive guide covers everything from single-celled organisms and dinosaurs to birds and mammals and the interplay between climate and man. Over 1,500 illustrations. 760pp. 7½ x 10⅛.   29371-8 Pa. $29.95

Prices subject to change without notice.

Available at your book dealer or write for free catalog to Dept. GI, Dover Publications, Inc., 31 East 2nd St., Mineola, N.Y. 11501. Dover publishes more than 500 books each year on science, elementary and advanced mathematics, biology, music, art, literary history, social sciences and other areas.